T0278780

TAR HOLLOW TRANS

TAR
HOLLOW TRANS

ESSAYS

STACY JANE GROVER

UNIVERSITY PRESS OF KENTUCKY

Scholarly publisher for the Commonwealth, serving Bellarmine University,
Berea College, Centre College of Kentucky, Eastern Kentucky University,
The Filson Historical Society, Georgetown College, Kentucky Historical Society,
Kentucky State University, Morehead State University, Murray State University,
Northern Kentucky University, Spalding University, Transylvania University,
University of Kentucky, University of Louisville, University of Pikeville, and
Western Kentucky University.
All rights reserved.

Editorial and Sales Offices: The University Press of Kentucky
663 South Limestone Street, Lexington, Kentucky 40508-4008
www.kentuckypress.com

Library of Congress Cataloging-in-Publication Data

Names: Grover, Stacy Jane, author.
Title: Tar Hollow trans : essays / Stacy Jane Grover.
Description: Lexington, Kentucky : The University Press of Kentucky, [2023]
   | Series: Appalachian futures: black, native, and queer voices | Includes
   bibliographical references.
Identifiers: LCCN 2022060214 | ISBN 9780813197555 (hardcover) |
   ISBN 9780813197692 (pdf) | ISBN 9780813197708 (epub)
Subjects: LCSH: Grover, Stacy Jane. | Transgender people—Ohio—Biography. |
   Gender identity--Ohio.
Classification: LCC HQ77.8.G36 A3 2023 | DDC 306.76/8092
   [B]—dc23/eng/20230110
LC record available at https://lccn.loc.gov/2022060214

Member of the Association
of University Presses

For Sonny Palmer

Nicht im Feld und auf den Bäumen—
In den Herzen muss es keimen,
Wenn es besser werden soll!

You cannot become better in the fields nor the trees—
the seed must germinate in the heart
if you want to become better.

—GOTTFRIED KELLER
"Regen-Sommer" (1846). Translated by Elizabeth Keith.

Contents

INTRODUCTION

I began this project as an exercise in trying to write myself into a heritage and identity that I had only recently discovered. I had begun a master's degree and was searching for an area to direct my research. My home region, this place called Appalachia, was suggested to me. At the time, I didn't think I had Appalachian heritage. I labeled my upbringing *rural* or *country*, although the area in which I grew up was not considered all that rural because there were places nearby that were always more rural, the *actual* country.

This disconnect stems partially from the fact that the county in which I grew up, for various reasons, does not appear on the Appalachian Regional Commission list. The label literally wasn't there. The Appalachian people lived a county over, in the hills, past some invisible line only minutes away. We seemed to share all the problematic issues—drugs, poverty, illiteracy, environmental degradation, brain and resource drain—but none of the culture.

I set out to research this missing background, to learn about myself and my family history, and maybe find a new way to relate to the world. I hadn't even identified as country or rural until I moved to a big city and realized just how nonmetropolitan I was. I wanted to see if the moniker *Appalachian* fit me.

This research brought deep insight to my memories and helped me make sense of so much that had seemed peculiar about my life. *Appalachian* gave a name to the sociocultural environment I grew up in: not fully rural, Ohio, or Midwest, but not West Virginia— and not the South, although kind of. But the harmony between my experience and the way of life described in books and studies and articles about Appalachia rapidly grew dissonant. In the light of all the tradition, heritage, and folkways contained within the mythic mountain range, my life seemed so very un-Appalachian. Yet the Appalachia of books read like a caricature.

At the same time, I had begun writing and publishing personal essays, and I was looking for new essay ideas. As I investigated the region, I found cultural artifacts, folkways, and historical tidbits that I considered relevant and interesting. Most of my writing had focused on being transgender, and I found resonance between how I felt about that identity and the feelings I encountered reading about Appalachia. I did not fit into the transgender scenes and culture of the major cities I moved to. They had never felt connected to my transgender life in the country, and they never clicked once I moved. I had failed to find the community promised in the very LGBTQIA-friendly Columbus—consistently ranked as one of the best cities in the nation in this regard—and yet my supposedly normative rural upbringing had supplied so much of a sense of community. I became invested in learning how my transgender existence informed and was informed by my upbringing in southeast Ohio, considering this nascent Appalachian identity. I wanted to find the missing piece of my belonging.

On a more superficial level, I knew that essays connecting personal identities with larger sociopolitical dialogues were popular, especially ones that explored themes like identity, trauma, childhood, place, class, gender, and sexuality. I had also tumbled into writing during a frenzied media revival of stereotypical, largely negative narratives about Appalachia, countered by a huge wave of new works celebrating and defending the region in the wake of the 2016 presidential election and the publication of a certain memoir by an author from my state.

So I decided I'd write a book exploring my transness through these new-to-me Appalachian cultural traditions and my Appalachian identity through transgender history and theory using the artifacts I discovered along the way as metaphors to frame my essays. At a time when popular personal essays follow a specific script—revealing personal anecdote, pop culture reference, connection to personal trauma, Google search for interesting facts, epiphany—I knew the framing sounded clever and interesting. That is, I knew the idea would sell.

Yet when I tried to write the project as planned, I found myself deeply disappointed in myself and dissatisfied with my writing. The identities of queer Appalachian or transgender Appalachian didn't ease the dissonance and confusion I felt reading about my home region, and those identity categories couldn't make my past self more legible to me. I couldn't fuse myself together, no matter what narrative and theoretical tricks I had at my disposal. My wish for different narratives outweighed my desire to write entertaining and properly plotted personal narratives following the popular script. And deep down, I didn't want to find myself represented in Appalachian or transgender writing. I wanted something more.

I set out instead to write a book that looked beyond representation to become a series of essays that chart my internal process of attempting and failing to rewrite my past to fit into identities and practices I've never claimed. To do this, I traced all the ways I've turned to fraught concepts like tradition, solidarity, community, and family—terms that dominate transgender and Appalachian discourses—to provide comfort and order in my life but come up empty and wanting. This book became an attempt to write honestly on the page, even at the expense of a properly narrated or entertaining story.

I encountered three interlocking challenges in writing this book. The first was how to write personal essays that resisted flattening author and text, substituting the very real complex me with the persona portrayed on the page. Because the experiences I relate happened in the past, they are reconstructed through story, and the stories we tell tend to follow certain standard narrative forms we've all inherited. Our self in the story becomes a character who relives our experiences through literary techniques of plot, setting, emotional heightening, and dramatic arcs. In crafting personal narratives, we scaffold our memories with as many verifiable facts as possible and reconstruct versions of ourselves on the page that best convey how the time we are narrating felt. We try to impart our subjective truth to the reader.

Often, maybe because of a lack of understanding of the genre, readers might interpret the self on the page as the author themselves rather than a literary device used in service of a mission. And easily accessible online personal essay and memoir writing in the past decade has only intensified this misunderstanding. Jia Tolentino, the author of *Trick Mirror: Reflections in Self Delusion* and staff writer at the *New Yorker,* has covered this development. In "The Personal-Essay Boom Is Over," she writes that "the online personal essay began to harden into a form defined by identity and adversity—not despite how tricky it is to negotiate those matters in front of a crowd but precisely because of that fact." Tolentino posits that this transformation came from the confluence of the growth and rise in popularity of social blogs and media platforms, online literary magazines, and online advertisements, especially the cost-per-click revenue system.

The more that authors of personal essays revealed their inner lives on the page, the more that readers flocked to these pieces, the more the essays were shared, the more revenue the magazine earned, and the more editors sought out this kind of personal essay. The difference between the personal essay as literary form and personal blogging for the sake of sharing the intimate details of one's life with others online collapsed.

Maybe because of this conflation, when readers discover that an author used a persona or changed events, settings, and names slightly to protect themselves and others in the story or used literary technique rather than simply presenting facts to better convey the truth of the experience, personal essays and memoirs—and by extension a writer's experiences—can be labeled as suspicious or even fraudulent. The distance and protection that writing a persona offer fail, and the writer is vulnerable to critique. As Tolentino writes, "Personal essays cry out for identification and connection; what their authors often got was distancing and shame." Our work betrays our mission.

The ways we're taught to read and understand literature in the United States only exacerbate this incongruence. Readers are generally taught that a text contains no stable meaning, and that the power to interpret the text lies with the reader—often through the technique of deconstructive reading. The importance and validity of the author's intention in crafting a work rank below the privileged position of reader critique. When there is no distinction between the true self and the persona in the text, authors themselves become rhetorical figures that can be read and interpreted. The power of representation, of meaning, falls to the reader, who knows the "true meaning" of the text. For marginalized writers who make meaning of and position themselves in the world through self-narration and self-representation, this erasure does real damage. Readers can bend the meaning of our stories to contradict us or deny our agency. Readers can rewrite or invalidate our experiences. Transgender writers like me, to paraphrase the transfeminist scholar Viviane Namaste, can so easily become the objects of study and never the subjects of history.

With this project, I sought to recover my memories and emotions as they happened, so I didn't want to use a persona on the page. Therefore, in each essay I had to carefully articulate and make meaning of my experiences in ways that left little room for interpretation. In many cases I had to tell instead of show. I let the me of the past remain unruly, resist my attempts to capture or represent or interpret her, restoring her agency. I placed her experiences and feelings above mine, which allowed me to self-narrate and self-represent in ways I couldn't have had I subjected my past self to my authorial wishes.

Because of this, the essays in this book often start and stop, circle back on themselves, cut off in the middle of a memory, or resist any meaningful self-interpretation altogether. This type of writing makes for stories that don't follow standard narrative arcs, ones that leave less room for ambiguity, less room to be read otherwise. Restoring agency to my past helped me to avoid turning my past self into a character onto whom my authorial self could bestow a legible history.

The second challenge I encountered writing this book was how to privilege resonance over taxonomy—that is, shared feeling over the shared experiences, values, or views that align with identity categories. I didn't believe my memories or feelings after my education in mainstream queer theory bulldozed over my past and replaced feelings with ideas. I was left with the ability to read my experiences like a text. I was full of answers and interpretations, and the ability to translate everything into something knowable, something manageable. But I wanted to recapture the feeling of being a child, of growing up in my home, of *being* in ways that run counter to, forsake, or make irrelevant the group identities I had tried to write myself into, whether Appalachian, queer, transgender, or even a representative member of my family. I wanted to again be so very unsure.

Privileging affect over taxonomy allows us to find resonance between our lives and the lives of others without having to take up the position of the other—to find parallel experiences or views. We don't have to find ourselves represented in the stories of others to understand or engage with them. Resonance allows us to find what decolonial feminist scholar Macarena Gómez-Barris calls a "viewpoint that comes from within—rather than from above, in relation to, or near." Aligning ourselves with rigid identity categories "buries the subtlety and complexity of the life force of the worlds that lie within." Privileging resonance over representation helps to maintain a "high biodiversity" in ourselves, the lives about which we write, and the ways of knowing embodied in them.

The third challenge I encountered was how to write criticism as creative praxis. I wanted to find a way to critique all that I wrote through—Appalachian, transgender, queer, and rural studies, academic theories, the essay as form—without performing criticism for criticism's sake, without uncovering, tearing down, or revealing without uplifting, pointing toward, or providing a way forward. In her book *Against Interpretation*, Susan Sontag offers a sharp criticism of literary interpretation that cut to the heart of this challenge and wove back through the previous two.

Sontag argues that instead of interpreting a text in a way that adds layers of meaning and context to what is already there, literary interpretation "excavates, and as it excavates, destroys; it digs 'behind' the text to find a sub-text which is the true one." This type of interpretation is "reactionary and stifling" and destroys our artistic sensibilities. She writes that "in a culture whose already classical dilemma is the hypertrophy of the intellect at the expense of energy and sensual capability, interpretation is the revenge of the intellect upon art." To interpret, in short, is "to deplete the world in order to set up a shadow world of meaning." The process of interpretation reduces art to its content, and once the content can be manipulated, much of the sensuousness of the art, the untranslatability, is lost, meaning the art can be "tamed" and "made manageable, comfortable." Sontag did not think that works of art cannot be described or discussed, but that we must develop a vocabulary to do so, one that is "descriptive rather than prescriptive," focusing on the form of the work instead of its supposed content.

Sontag's essay ends with a question that has indelibly shaped my thinking around both writing and criticism: "What would criticism look like that would serve the work of art, not usurp its place?" The aim of criticism should be to make art and the experiences that inform it more real to us than they were previously. Criticism should show "how [something] is what it is, even, that it is what it is, rather than . . . show what it means." Therefore, criticism should focus on what a writer tries to express and how they've expressed it, and in the process should interrogate the self as closely as it does the text.

To solve these challenges, I set out to show my experiences as they were for what they were, and to write through what I was encountering and not against it, though I worried whether the criticism I produced would sully the creative expression rather than support it. This question is one that writer and cultural anthropologist Ruth Behar discusses in *The Vulnerable Observer: Anthropology That Breaks Your Heart.*

> I think what we are seeing are efforts to map an intermediate space we can't quite define yet, a borderland between passion and intellect, analysis and subjectivity, ethnography and autobiography, art and life. . . . The anxiety around such works is that it will prove to be beyond criticism, that it will be undiscussable. But the real problem is that we need other forms of criticism, which are rigorous yet not disinterested; forms of criticism which are not immune to catharsis; forms of criticism which can respond vulnerably, in ways we must begin to try to imagine.

Behar calls for more honest ways of being in and documenting our world, which begin with recognizing how our personal and cultural worldviews shape our interactions with the world and the meaning we construct from it. Bringing our feeling selves forward, allowing ourselves to be open and vulnerable and dwelling in this uncomfortable space helps us to be more honest and to write more honestly.

To begin imagining new forms of criticism, I needed not only to construct a passive mental formation of what I wished for my writing but also to summon all that my body remembered and sensed in what Mary Anglin calls an "act of imagination." Imagination as an act required vulnerability, required that I didn't seek to master what I perceived but to respond in ways that allowed me to move and be moved by all that I encountered. I needed a method to negotiate these challenges and write this book.

The poet and scholar Alexis Pauline Gumbs provided a guidebook for me. In trying to write *Spill: Scenes of Black Feminist Fugitivity,* a book engaging with Hortense Spillers's body of work, Gumbs had to devise a new analytic, and the analytic she chose was love. In an interview about writing the book, she states that "Because of love, I sought a methodology that would allow me to write *with* Spillers instead of continuing to merely write *about* her work. The difference between *about* and *with* has to do with intimacy, conspiracy; maybe we can call that love. Some people call it 'we go together.'" Love transforms who we are, the way we think and feel, and causes us to act. Love changes our lives. Love resists categorization and by doing so provides a method of writing *with* myself, *with* the past, *with* my family, *with* the region.

Maintaining an embodied vulnerability and intimacy *with* all that I engaged allowed me to write with love for myself as a figure from the past who deserves agency and with love for my family, whose stories deserve to be told but whose lives deserve opacity. I could write through being transgender without turning myself into a symbol, without writing stereotypical narratives—or, if my experiences happened to align with these stereotypes, I didn't judge myself for that. Love allowed me to want better for transgender existence, for my home region and its people, for the landscape, and for those whose work I read and those who read my work.

Writing with love became a central tenet of the nine essays in this book. Although my voice fills these pages, my voice is not isolated because the memories I shape into stories were co-created. While I explore multiple topics—folkways, archives, artifacts, traditions, academic theories, the landscape, transgender existence—I don't write as an expert. I am contemplating rather than arguing. I'm imagining that a future exists in which terms like *transgender* and *Appalachian* might lose all reference and meaning, a future in which we can restore a complex interiority to our lives.

I open and close the book with essays of hope because in the end it might be all I have, but the middle is a long and uncertain passage. In some essays I'm sure of myself and in others I waver. I contradict myself on my thoughts, memories, and emotions. In some places I lose faith in writing as a vehicle to express myself, and in others I find that the essay helps me unfold the sensuous experience of finding myself. I take the challenges I faced head-on and lose myself in them.

This work is a record of my thinking, a recovery attempt, a compendium of my disappointment, an archive of my failure. These essays are an act of solidarity, an act of striving to find wonder. Here is a vulnerable work—prone to catharsis, unmanageable, uncomfortable, bewildering, enchanted—that strives to explore the self as much as the world she inhabits. Here is an act of imagination, an act of love.

I invite you to write yours.

LANCASTER IS BURNING

I see a city marked by flame. On East Main Street, General Sherman's childhood home stands as a museum. Every day pickup trucks with Confederate flags in the back windows blast by in mushroom clouds of diesel smoke. Lancaster takes pride in being the birthplace of the man who cut across the South, leaving only ashes in his wake. The story of the great field burner and the many legacies fire left on this place have been seared into us since childhood. Ebenezer Zane blazed a trail from Pennsylvania to Kentucky, founding the first white settler villages. The first Anchor Hocking glass factory burned to the ground and resumed production only six months later, naming its most famous product line Fire King. The Fairfield County Fair—the longest continually running fair in Ohio—was famous for such events as "Racing by Gas Light" and the "Lake of Fire." I carry these histories with me as I wander through town. I see them everywhere.

Down the street, the grandstand in the fairgrounds smolders. The grandstand, built in 1909 and featured in the finale of the 1948 film *Green Grass of Wyoming*, was destroyed by arson in a single night. As I stare at the rubble, I remember the words spoken by George Ward Nichols, Sherman's aide-de-camp, as he saw Atlanta burning: "A grand and awful spectacle is presented to the beholder in this beautiful city, now in flames."

Across town, smoke looms large and black above Anchor Hocking's clamshell as the factory burns again. Firefighters on extended ladders discharge water from hoses to quench the billowing flames. Seeing them, I am reminded again of Sherman and his response to President Lincoln's call to send more troops to fight the Confederacy:

"Why, you might as well attempt to put out the flames of a burning house with a squirt-gun."

On King Street lie the remnants of a house exploded by a basement meth lab. The spires of brick towering over the blackened hills of rubble carry fragrant memory upward from the stones below.

On the occasion of this fortuitous homecoming, of seeing my birthplace in flames, I ponder the nature of self, of place. I haven't inhabited—occupied, lived in, been present in, or taken up space in—this town for years. And while the town never fled the corridors of my bodily memory, I fled it. The landscape of Fairfield County, Ohio sprouted the seeds of my imagination, helped them take root. I created my own worlds in which myriad lives were lived among the very real rich and varied Appalachian characters with whom I shared my life. My father levitated at church. My mother foresaw her grandmother's house burning down. My grandmother braved a barn fire to save a horse. The women of my family were sensitive, always seeming to know more than what was visible, impossibly wise to me as a young child. I dreamed of inheriting their strength and wisdom, and in many ways I did. I dressed and played how I chose, hidden by the trees and valleys that surrounded me, unencumbered by the terrible burden of gender. Without any references to compare myself to, without any knowledge of others who felt or thought like me, I assumed everyone did. I had the vague sense that my queerness was a mark, but it was mine and I wore it well. It took the shapes I formed it in, filling the empty spaces of fields, dancing in the shadows between forests, falling freely down rolling hills deep into the sandstone valleys below.

I was a shy girl whose mind was shaped by the geography even as the geography was irreparably being shaped around me. As trees were removed for roads, fields for houses, barns for garages, so too was my own imagination replaced by an overgrowth of new information. I encountered stereotypes of the rural women I idolized that portrayed them reductively as strong, fierce preservers of rural culture, matriarchs with otherworldly attachments to the land, or as poor victims, battered, subservient wives struggling to raise children. The best of them were the beautiful but dumb, available girls with strong sexual appetites. I inherited a new way of seeing from these negative portrayals. I began seeing the women around me differently. I began seeing myself differently, too.

When I came out as transgender and searched for a community, I struggled, wishing to be a country woman, of the land, that place of undefined gender, to not leave the landscape behind in embracing my newfound identity. But I did not want to be a victim: battered, subservient. I didn't want to endure more than I had endured. The small queer community I found told me I had to leave the suffocating myopia of the countryside to experience true freedom, and the deaths of Brandon Teena and Matthew Shepard—the first visible manifestations of queerness I had encountered—only reinforced in my mind that the only good queer in the country was a dead one. Rural life and queer life were simply incompatible. With nothing to hold onto, no strength to reference, I gave up trying to affirm myself, burying my feelings in the soil deep beneath sedimentary layers of red clay and limestone. I felt trapped, as though the mountains were threatening to collapse and bury me beneath them. I had to get away, put distance between me and this town, as if my problems were tied up in the landscape, the sacred forests of my memory, as if the geography that shaped me was suddenly my undoing.

I moved to the state capital, where I found not the expected freedom but constraint, not the promised anonymity that would allow fluidity in my expressions but constant surveillance. I inherited a new queerness, one that was now a mark I was told how to wear, shaping me into contours I didn't recognize. I was what was restraining my transformation, and to grow into the shared vision of metropolitanism that would lead to my salvation, I left behind all that the country planted in me. That seeing stars was a part of being, that horizons were literal, that backwards was a direction that most often led to family, that sunsets couldn't be blocked by anything but mountains and only if one decided not to climb them—these things I could not bring into the dusty confines of the metropolis. The brick and wire and concrete hardened any permeable part of my mind, kept out the climate that shaped me, the person I had been among the fields and trees and valleys of my childhood.

Walking through this landscape now, my memory map morphs as landmarks I encounter remind me not of a place in stasis—mythically free or myopically restrictive—but of an ecosystem in constant flux.

In each ecosystem fire behaves differently, and organisms within them must adapt accordingly. The characteristics of how fire interacts with a given ecosystem is called a fire regime. Fires burn at three levels: ground, surface, and crown. Ground fires burn through the soil that is rich in organic matter. Surface fires burn through dead plant material on the ground. Crown fires burn in the tops of shrubs and trees. Organisms that live within these regimes are either resistant, tolerant, or intolerant to these types of fires. The places within an ecosystem ravaged by fire range from freshly burned spaces to locations fire has left untouched for years. Sites burned by fire progress through continuous and directional phases of colonization that are characterized by the vegetation that arises. After a fire, the seeds already present in the soil—or seeds that can travel quickly to the soil—will be the first to regrow in the burned space. Different species of plants can exploit different stages in the colonization process, creating in the landscape patches of multiple species. The unique makeup of these patches is determined by the characteristics—soil, climate, and topography—of a place, characteristics in constant flux.

There are spaces in town where fire has burned enough for me to inhabit them. The antique store, that catacomb of consumerism's past where beauty and embarrassment fetch equally dubious prices, whose wares are displayed in unflattering, dust-drenched, wood-paneled crypts. I fit in here, somewhere between the state spoon collections, the mid-century furniture, the mannequins that, like me, stand strangely overdressed, catching double glances by passersby who know the proportions aren't quite right. I can hide here among these queer items queerly out of time.

The coffee shop in the old hardware store on Broad Street, its décor more out of place than me, demanding more attention than I can garner. Giant paintings of Santa Claus praying in sanctuaries hang from the exposed brick, distracting gazes away from the table in the back corner where I sit with my coffee, reading, unnoticed for hours.

The alley behind the old record store where I first kissed the boy with the blondest hair wearing orange parachute pants and candy bracelets who waited for me holding sushi. Giving shade for over a century, thick moss meets brick street where few cars pass and few feet bother to tread the uneven ground. I sit alone, daydreaming, unburdened from the necessity of constant attention to my surroundings.

There are spaces where the fire has barely touched, and these I can inhabit only fleetingly. The fountain square at night, where I can sit and look up at the clock tower through the tree branches. The silence expands the town enough to include me. I can't stay long, for daytime brings families, children, businesspeople—relational categories of existence that, when present, erase mine. But for a while, the water is all mine; the cherub faces gaze only at me.

In Rising Park, the green surrounding Standing Stone, where nature offers refuge but also a seclusion that allows for violence. I hide off the regular paths, my feet finding comfort in uncertain terrain. The view from the mountaintop shrinks the town so that I'm able to include it within me. I savor what I can before moving on, careful to notice those around me.

The west side of town by the factories, what Dickens might have described as the "neutral ground upon the outskirts of the town which was neither town nor country, and yet was either spoiled." The gaps in the railroad tracks and power lines, the holes in the fences, the cracks in the crumbling foundations give me room to breathe, to think, to create. Yet the isolation leaves me unprotected. I keep moving, never stopping long enough to be seen.

There are spaces where the fire has not touched, and in these I find little or no space. The grocery store under the unforgiving incandescence. I go at night and park close to avoid the jaundice light of the parking lot, the groups of men and their cars gathered at the edges, the aggressive machismo brewing trouble. I hit the needed aisles with precision, never strolling with Ginsburg or Whitman, feet always moving, head always down.

Independence Day at the fairgrounds, where the throng of bodies moving in close quarters squeezes out that which doesn't fit the mold. The combination of feverish nationalism and alcohol becomes a potent mix that never fails to combust. I watch from afar, reminiscing of a youth spent sprawled on quilts staring past the red-chipped barn roofs into a coarse July sky.

The mall, the microcosm of consumerism's worst traits illuminated by piercing fluorescence and hard, unwelcoming floors. The building contains my body, hyper-visible, unable to escape the gazes of others or the memories amassed in a decade of working here. I won't risk going.

I circle back through town, breathing in the smoke from so many fires. The smoke has seeped into my hair, my pores, the fabric of me. The thick scent conjures faded bodily memories, summons in me the realization that no matter how I've tried to erase the traces of this place, the Ohio country has stuck like pollen to every inch of me. No matter how I've changed or tried to wipe the dust of wheat and corn from my being, I can't. The mountains have opened my senses to a different way of knowing, of being, so that no matter where I go or who I encounter, I weave them into the quilt of my past.

Lancaster weaves into a patchwork before me, the fires burning holes that provide glimpses of pathways regrown and growing, membranes seeping and spilling, the ecosystem pulsating, glimpses of eternity. I know the story of this place is not a linear trajectory, not the narratives inherited from my ancestors, the writing of will onto landscape. The land is the land is the land, and while it has never been open, it has opened me.

In Rising Park, four hundred people spread out under trees and by the many ponds, commemorating the county's first Pride parade and celebration. The unusually cool Ohio June—free of rain and its usual high humidity—helps the celebrants relax, let down guards so habitually worn, guards that often keep them from participating in, let alone appreciating, the daily spaces they inhabit. When it is even possible, relaxing in the summer often brings anxiety, fear, and violence to those unable to shield themselves inside, away from other bodies and the necessity of light dress. The day carries a peaceful density that cuts through the usual tension. No protestors come to intimidate; no preachers with bullhorns come to shame. For an afternoon, the tension rages on outside the confines of these bodies melded in hill, shade, and tree. And in the center of the park, by the largest pond, a new tree sprouts in the shade of old ones, finding room among all that is already present, the nascent result of eons of soil, climate, and topography, the creation of the flux.

A Position Which Is Nowhere

The hog snorted, blasting a plume of dust and hay and debris over the bristles of its face. The pig trembled, squealing, fighting to get away from the rope binding it to the wooden pole in the ground. A dread, a wrongness, unfurled, blinding: Peter's unclean sheet. The slaughtering of a hog wasn't supposed to arouse this kind of feeling. If anything, it should have given her an expansive feeling, an incandescent, pulsating connection back to the Flood, before the Flood—but, like God before he wiped all but two of each animal from the Earth, she grieved—her heart filled with pain. She could not kill it, couldn't even watch; the sheet could never be clean, the second mandate never fulfilled.

At sixteen years old, Bessie had been well accustomed to the rhythms of the farm, the noise and grit and death. Every year on the first frost of winter, her daddy led the slaughtering and processing of hogs for family and neighbors. Traditionally, all who had hogs ready to slaughter brought as many as they had, sometimes up to one hundred, fattened on peas, corn, potatoes, and mast from wood. Everyone would gather before dawn to place large stones on an open fire to heat barrels of water. The hogs were killed, bled, scalded, then hung on a gambrel, where their hair was scraped off. The hogs were cooled overnight, then cut up and salted the next day. Hams, jaws, shoulders, heads, and sides were packed separately on a tilted platform off the ground of a smokehouse. Brine was caught in troughs underneath the pigs, which was later boiled down and evaporated so the pork salt could be used for cooking. Hog-killing day provided fresh meat, cured hams, fat, and brine for the whole community.

Bessie should have been able to help with the killing of hogs. Her reputation for toughness was known countywide. People said she could build a fence as fast and with as much accuracy as two men doing the same work. She could sharpshoot and pigeon shoot better than any of the boys in the area. She could lift a man over her shoulder and carry him for a hundred yards. She knew how to fix a car. The crops she planted never failed. She worked hard at Buchanan's restaurant and roomed upstairs during the school year so she could study instead of work on the farm. She had dreams for college. And when she was eventually shot in the head on a September night in 1922, she held on for four days in the hospital before she died.

Bessie's genuine humility and beauty only bolstered her tough reputation. The newspapers noted that she "had a fine character," and the local sheriff said she was "kind, helpful, didn't drink, and stayed out of trouble." In her sophomore year she was voted "most pretty" in her 1922 high school yearbook. Bessie's inability to kill an animal for dinner was just another unique trait, a compassion that God rarely designed. In everyone's estimation, she seemed above reproach and humiliation.

Beatrice spoke quietly, using her hands to fill in the words she couldn't think of or to gesture toward a listener to supply the missing words, which we all rushed to do, jumping up onto our knees or feet, shouting. I stared up at Beatrice's dark sunglasses. The room quieted around her as everyone leaned in to hear her soft voice. As she spoke, we laughed and shushed each other, put hands over mouths, reached for others, and gestured for quiet, pointer fingers raised to pursed lips.

I pulled my knees under me, leaving a flat, light trail in the brown shag carpet. My cousins sat beside me, cross-legged, on their knees, or flat on the floor as the adults sat on the furniture or stood leaning on walls around the room. My great-grandmother Beatrice sat in the recliner at the center of the room, her dogs in her lap, their eyes and ears rising and falling at the motion around them.

Every year on Christmas Eve, we gathered at Beatrice's house and listened to her tell family stories. Some of the stories we'd heard a dozen times; some only she remembered. Some were subject to contentious interpretations that would lead to lengthy discussions. That time, I asked her about Bessie and the room fell silent. Bessie was Beatrice's sister-in-law, my grandfather William's sister. Bessie was murdered at sixteen and her death was a painful hole in the family tree. We all knew the story, but I liked hearing Beatrice tell it.

I listened to Beatrice and the older relatives discuss the details of Bessie's life and her untimely death. The women sitting in the room all resembled Beatrice. I looked around at their round faces, their dark hair, their deep-set eyes, their rising cheekbones. I wanted nothing more than to grow up and become like them. I craved their deep belly laughs, the wisdom and closeness they shared from decades of living and working together.

I found the women of my family extraordinary. They were farm hands who raised horses and worked in addition to homemaking. All were mothers. Beatrice was the mother of eleven, grandmother of thirty-four, and great-grandmother of twelve when she died just before my generation started having children. They were nurturing women who pooled resources to care for the vast array of kin. They maintained homes, farms, gardens, and animals, cooked and cleaned, lived and breathed the family. They were women I respected, maybe feared a little, women who made me want to do and be better.

I spent my time trying to absorb all their kind but demanding teaching offered. I learned the particulars of how to care for a home, how to clean and keep hardwood floors, how to use vinegar and newspapers on the windows, how to deodorize with baking soda, how to clean the cobwebs from the ceilings but leave the spiders, which took care of the bugs. I learned to wash and fold laundry and the ways of removing various stains from different fabrics. In the kitchen, I stood beside my grandmother on a chair, then on the floor when I was tall enough, and helped her sauté, fry, and season. I paid close attention as she carefully preserved the bacon grease in a coffee can she kept under the sink, mixing the old oil with flour when she threw it out. I learned to make and mend clothing.

I wanted to work with my hands, care for others, laugh and love as hard as they did, and I felt myself falling in place beside my girl cousins as we learned from the women. We played together in the woods, in the barns, with the animals. We played dress-up and house. We imagined our future families—our weddings, our children's names, how we'd redecorate the houses we grew up in, so sure that we would never leave them.

Yet as I grew older, little by little something new began to take over. While cooking, cleaning, taking care of children, playing with cousins, rolling dough in the kitchen with my grandmother, mowing the yard, a hole would open in the forested hillside and I'd fall through. A great invisible and unnamed magnetic force pulled me and everything around me down.

At first I felt the force as a dull ache, a gnawing phantom that haunted only me. But as the years passed, the force seemed to possess the women in my family too. When I took my place in the kitchen with my aunts and cousins, suddenly my aunts would speak quietly in a kind of code I didn't know, or they would whisper into my girl cousins' ears and they would laugh. They'd gesture toward the men in the family and speak about things that I suddenly seemed unwittingly included in. I could feel the shadow that grew over them spreading. They'd all transformed. Something had happened and they had to whisper around me or leave the room to speak to one another. The men whispered too, but I overheard their words directly: *Something's not right with that kid.*

What happened, what changed so that I felt excluded where I had always felt I belonged? Was I doing something wrong? After these experiences, I observed the girls in my family carefully. I embodied their mannerisms, the tones they spoke in, their bodily comportment, but the shadow that had come between us only grew darker. I was no longer one of them.

To shield myself from the strange force, I tried to fit in with the boys. I observed the boys' strange behaviors and rituals, especially when they weren't around girls. Girls were suddenly off limits, not friends. And they talked about them in such awful ways, like they weren't really people but existed only in relation to what they wanted from them, usually expressed in crass jokes about sex, or at least the idea of sex, what they learned from the magazines and photos they found on the internet. They devised plans to see girls in various stages of undress.

I joined the boys in their activities. I tried to toughen up and play sports. I attended Boy Scouts for one ill-fated meeting and then never went back to that basement full of boys and their fathers. The boys talked loudly over one another with a force that upset me, but they didn't notice. I liked cars but didn't know any of their details. I didn't race dirt bikes or idolize sports figures like Dale Earnhardt, whose death was the only tragedy I ever saw bring my uncle to tears. I didn't fit in with the boys and I didn't want to, yet I was ever increasingly pushed toward them, and it hurt me.

For the purpose of the obvious narrative I'm building, I could name the shadow that kept me from ever touching a properly gendered childhood *dysphoria* or use some other jargon—*compulsory-sexual-or-gender-something*. If I turn to my training in gender studies and theory, I know that this gendering force wasn't particular to me, my family, or the place in which I grew up. It was the everyday, often invisible manifestations of the social and cultural forces of a time of suspicion growing out of the final crumbling of the Cold War era. All this turmoil could be blamed on the countless evil people in the world, the monsters looking to tear society apart. This paranoid hunt for hidden monsters often led to an increased focus on how women and girls—for their protection—were perceived in emerging and shifting understandings of femininity.

By the 1970s, these forces broadly condensed into two competing views. One was the conservatism that sought a return to the patriarchal, heterosexual, cisgender nuclear family. Women had earned social, legal, and economic rights, and armed with these new freedoms and in response to the economic downturn, they began to work away from home and have fewer children, trends many saw as contributing to the death of the American Dream. At the same time, women's discontent regarding patriarchy, misogyny, and general lack of resources and care was boiling over. What womanhood meant in relation to men's authority was in question. Womanhood as a category was simultaneously expanding and shrinking.

These competing forces found a scapegoat that both sides could blame for all gendered societal problems. After decades of activism that led to increasing gains in rights and visibility, transgender women posed a problem to the national social order. Medical technology was creating women with bodies that seemed to defy nature. People who opposed transgender women portrayed them as deviant sex fiends, monstrous, unnatural, and unfit to be either wives or mothers. We threatened the nuclear family and the safety of women and girls.

This suspicion and distrust grew to a frenzy in the decade before my birth, culminating most infamously in the 1979 publication of Janice Raymond's book *The Transsexual Empire*. In the name of feminism, Raymond painted transgender women as another threat to cisgender women, as men who were playing women to infiltrate women's spaces to dominate them psychically and physically. In this illogic, sexism was a social problem, and instead of fixing the social problem through education and behavioral modification, the medical establishment was subverting feminism's gains by forming an "empire" of transsexuals ready to dominate cisgender women and render them obsolete. To Raymond and her ilk, the gender monster was under the bed, waiting to attack the woman or child sleeping on it.

This rhetoric shaped how the medical and legal establishments treated trans women, lending authority to anti-trans sentiment. Gender affirmation surgeries as well as medical, psychological, and legal help for transsexuals came under intense scrutiny. Amid the fear that an evil empire was forming, the reality was that thousands of transgender women were being turned away from care. Shortly after the book's publication, the Catholic psychiatrist Paul McHugh shut down the famed Johns Hopkins gender clinic. It turned out that closing the clinic had been his goal since he took over the directorship.

In an interview published in the *New York Times,* McHugh said that his "personal feeling is that surgery is not a proper treatment for a psychiatric disorder, and it's clear to me that these patients have severe psychological problems that don't go away following surgery." McHugh and many in psychiatry at the time saw transsexual people as depressed and isolated individuals with profound dependency issues.

Thus the medical establishment became gatekeepers to whom trans women had to plead for their existence. This establishment created and enforced strict rules limiting who qualified for access to care. These rules centered on a narrow set of diagnostic criteria designed to filter out the large swath of bad seeds, offering treatment only to people with a true "disorder"—and a healthy, attractive, small body that would have a chance of being perceived as cisgender after surgeries and hormones.

Even as gender clinics became places where a small group of heavily screened trans women could have their bodies transformed, the clinics operated as charm schools. What made a woman a woman was her performance of the gender—fitting in with the current socially sanctioned comportment, grooming, clothing, makeup, and hair styles for femininity—including her willingness to police other women's adoption of these norms. Men doctors dictated what made a good woman, and they taught transgender women to behave like their constructed version of the ideal.

The diagnostic criteria included a history of displeasure with the patient's current bodily form, unhappiness with the activities commonly assigned to the gender they were raised into, and generally an expression of wanting sexual partners of the gender opposite to the one they were to transition into. Doctors labeled transgender women unwell if they didn't improve themselves, continued to see therapists, remained unmarried, or had same-gender partners.

The result was that "being in the wrong body" became the main defining diagnostic criterion for being transsexual, and that the only care offered was "treatment" in the form of medical and social transition, so long as the person was a good candidate. This treatment logic was codified, for better or worse, in 1980 in the *Diagnostic and Statistical Manual of Mental Disorders* (*DSM*). "Transsexualism" was defined as a disorder characterized by "a persistent sense of discomfort and inappropriateness about one's anatomic sex and a persistent wish to be rid of one's genitals and to live as a member of the other sex." Transgender activists tried to have this listing removed—as homosexuality had been—but transsexualism continued to appear in later editions of the DSM. In 1994, while I was growing up, the name of the disorder changed to "gender identity disorder," but the definition remained largely the same—"a strong and persistent cross-gender identification."

Transgender women learned that if they wanted to access medical care, they had to carefully navigate the system. The main way of doing this was to construct and narrate life histories, constructed scripts, that made sense in the medical order. They knew they had to claim they were experiencing life in the wrong body, they found no pleasure in this body, and they believed their dysphoria and their concomitant emotional and/or physical issues would subside after medical care. Transgender women had to pass medical tests, pass life history interviews, be able to pass as cisgender, heterosexual women. Thus, the plausible histories of transness they constructed, based on the guidelines the system formulated, focused on passing. And the narrative of passing to the exclusion of all other narratives and ways of existing in the world reduced who a trans woman could be to a single category: one properly gendered performance, one script to follow.

Growing up, I wasn't passing as a girl, a boy, or even a tomboy, and I felt shame at my inability to navigate the invisible confines of my childhood. This shame rolled over the landscape deep into the very soil, the red clay, the roots of maple, beech, and sycamore, the wispy clouds of mycorrhizae beneath me. It grew into everything I did. I looked at my family and knew that I was not growing into their shapes. My roots had grown a tree that failed to bloom. I internalized this difference. I didn't know what to do with the shame I experienced in that space, so I left it to linger, to settle on everything in the landscape, kicked up in the haze of summer, the wet of spring pollen, the October rain that drenched the hills. I saw it in the fog of the creek bed, the little patch of sun-yellowed grass on the slope by the barn. I maneuvered around my shame or stayed away from it entirely. Through the echoes of "Something's not right with that kid" I knew my family could see how I kept to myself, the ways I sat quietly and observed before acting, the ways I failed to interact entirely. They were naming my shyness, the ways I fumbled through and around the invisible rules of the world.

Although I didn't consider it at the time, assigning shame as the cause of my shyness builds to something interesting narratively. I have a theoretical toolkit I can reach into to make this easy association. In *Touching Feeling: Affect, Pedagogy, Performativity*, gender studies scholar Eve Sedgwick writes, "Some persons who feel themselves most governed by shame find themselves labeled as 'shy.'" This shyness, she writes, is "the same kind of feeling that is made excessively visible in moments of awkward interpersonal exchange." So, armed now with this theory, I can look back and see that the way I interacted in the world was governed by the emotional experience of physically encountering my bodily difference, leading me to regulate, navigate, and organize my world around my shame. As I grew older, my shame sucked me back into that former time and kept a piece of me there.

If I follow this line of theoretical thinking and dig further into my training, I learn that I was stuck in this shame because I hadn't attended to or transformed it. The queer theorist Heather Love writes that recognizing and attending to shame is critical. Shame affects everyone. I can see shame in others, know that I'm not alone and what I'm going through is not unique to me. But leaving shame to linger without examining it makes it hard for me to notice this same shame in others. This leads to isolation, more shame, more shyness.

Again, I look back with this knowledge and see shame so clearly draped over my childhood. The force that pulled my kin and me apart was this shame, the invisible gendering forces of our lives. Some part of me might have known—or at least felt—that my family too was coming up against the confines of shame, but I couldn't name or acknowledge this. As we grew older, my girl cousins most likely took on the shame of being tomboys, of suddenly being expected to groom more and to pay attention to what boys wanted. My boy cousins had to spend less and less time with the girls. I'd see them men yell and scream at their softness, their vulnerability, like they did to me. I can now so clearly see them trapped in a forced inability to express themselves. We were all hurting and confused and expressing that by hurting one another. Yet I was caught in the middle of a shame that still didn't fit neatly with theirs, a gendered shame that turned me inward, looking for refuge.

At this point in the narrative, to make the story interesting I might have turned to stories of Bessie for comfort, as a template to challenge my unwieldy shame. I was obsessed with her life. I kept photos and newspaper clippings of accounts about her in a folder and made copies to hang on my walls and cut up into collages. I turned to her story often for reasons that didn't have anything to do with my gendered upbringing. But the evidence suggests that she seemed to exist somewhere between genders or outside of them. If she could avoid the trappings of gender, managing to straddle worlds, maybe I could too. With a little social and historical background into Bessie's time, I could turn my dead relative into a symbol for the sake of a believable personal narrative.

The transformation is easy to make. The archival and oral accounts attest that Bessie didn't fit the usual template of a rural white farm girl in the 1920s. In *4-H Harvest: Sexuality and the State in Rural America,* the historian Gabriel Rosenberg writes that poor white women in rural areas of the United States during Bessie's time were not well regarded for their abilities to build fences, wrangle animals, shoot guns, or farm. Social, cultural, and economic elements of the time—the farm crisis of the 1920s; the eugenics movement, which was fostered through the rural hygiene and modernization movements; and extension education such as 4-H and home economics—projected the perceived decay of the quintessential rural American way of life onto poor rural white women.

Prominent thinkers at the time, such as Gertrude Warren, the USDA's champion for girls' reform and mother of 4-H and home economics, and Orie Latham Hatcher, pioneer in vocational studies, argued that cities were draining the countryside of young men and women with the promise of work, freedom from parents, leisure activities, and the vices of sexual delinquency, drugs, and alcohol. The exodus of youth from the countryside to cities was dangerous not only because cities were sites of sexual impropriety, indecent activities, and inappropriate entertainment, but also because cities contained too many Black families and families of color reproducing too quickly, causing overpopulation. The flight of young, healthy white youth from the countryside threatened to topple the rural white nuclear family, the backbone of the nation.

Thinkers like Warren and Hatcher argued that one of the causes of this rural family crisis was that girls were leaving the countryside because they were being overworked at home. These thinkers, and the vast federally funded programs they organized, actively shamed women and girls for working outside the home or doing farm work, even when their labor meant economic stability and even though working the land meant remaining close to home.

In fact, rural white farm women in the 1920s were barely seen as women. Men especially castigated these women. Horace Kephart, travel writer and the rural everyman's favorite pseudo-sociologist, author of the infamous book *Our Southern Highlanders,* wrote about farm women: "Hard toil in house and field, early marriage, frequent child-bearing with shockingly poor attention, and ignorance or defiance of the plainest necessities of hygiene, soon warp and age them."

Similarly, Roy Hinman Holmes, a professor of sociology at the University of Michigan, described a farm girl in his 1922 book *The Farm in a Democracy*: she had a "tired, care worn look and might easily be taken for a little old woman, when in reality, she is just a few years past her teens." This girl and the young women on farms that these thinkers at the time wanted to save had "not had an opportunity to acquire womanly gracefulness, nor taste in dress," and their manners were "crude and awkward." Holmes noted that "young growing girls were called upon to perform duties entirely too heavy and strenuous," finishing with the most damning observation: "A man is not permitted to overload his horse or abuse his hired man but is permitted to overwork his children to satisfy a greed for profit." In 1923, a year after Bessie's death, the *Washington Post* ran an article with the headline "The Middle West Farm Woman of Today Is the Man of the Family." This was obviously not a compliment.

The rhetoric that rural white women lacked womanliness because they were drudges who farmed the land was built on a long-held anti-Black and anti-Indigenous settler colonial logic that categorized those who lived close to and worked the land as less than human. Black and Native women had been excluded from the category of *woman* from the very beginning—the discourse just took a while to catch up to rural white women. To white eugenicists, poor rural white women became symbols of social and biological backwardness unbefitting a strong, developing nation. These women were, however, redeemable.

This crisis was nothing the federal government couldn't solve with intensive investments and eugenicist scientific expertise. Medical experts, home economists, and extension educators like those from 4-H could enter the family life of rural society and change it from the inside. The best strategists of society and government turned to the problem of rural women to solve both their physical appearance and reproductive capacities, which would in turn help the home, the land, the community, the countryside, the nation.

To assist girls in transforming their bodies to make them fit for healthy reproduction, men health professionals subjected girls to intensive and invasive bodily scrutiny. Girls in 4-H were given scorecards listing potential bodily defects and providing guidelines for improvement. Health professionals, who were mostly men, would then inspect and score the girls and advise them on how to fix their defects to conform to eugenicist health guidelines. By 1930 more than one hundred thousand youth had undergone these examinations and health projects—90 percent of them girls.

Health and hygiene experts wanted to reduce the strenuous and unfeminine labor and activities that girls like Bessie took part in to concentrate on health, beauty, and hygiene, guided by the knowledge and help of objective and quantifiable expert advice. Girls were taught how to dress properly. Homemade, sturdy, functional clothing and shoes that could be repaired marked rural women as out of style. The mainstream ready-to-wear clothing industry, fashion magazines, and the advertisements created a standard body shape and size and sold readers the proper clothes to adorn it.

The goal was not only a beautiful and healthy girl but a refined one as well. Home economists and extension educators could teach girls proper femininity according to the ever-changing and restrictive definitions. Doing physically laborious work injured a girl's pride and self-respect and led her away from the refined fulfillment of homemaking. The rural home became a symbol for America itself. Home economics taught girls to pick out home furnishings that made their homes aesthetically pleasing. The health and hygiene of the home included nutritious, attractive meals that would bring health to their future family's bodies and peace to their minds. A happy home also included the ways women and girls comported themselves within it. Girls had to learn how to grow into proper women, and there was one script to follow.

By all accounts, Bessie seemed to follow a different script, one in which she could farm, go to school, and keep herself beautiful, fashionable, and healthy. She could do what both boys and girls did, and it seems as though everyone loved her for it. If I braid her story with mine, I can make a grand narrative of gender triumph. Connecting her story with mine transforms her into the gender rebel, the ultimate tomboy symbol to resolve my dissonance. Portraying Bessie as my mythic mountain woman ancestor allows me to draw an unbroken line that extends from the very hills themselves to me.

I know there is a tendency for stigmatized people to look to the past to ancestors' stories of resistance, survival, and defiance to guide us. And I know this impulse has consequences. In *Feeling Backwards: Loss and the Politics of Queer History,* the queer theorist Heather Love cautions against this search. She writes that by placing the shame, hardship, and defiance of figures from the past "in a positive genealogy of gay identity, we make good on their suffering, transforming their shame into pride after the fact." This transformation makes what people in the past experienced seem inevitable, somehow worth it. They had to go through what they did so that we can have something now. Even though their supposed struggles through shame were not the whole of their experiences, we can pluck out that one narrative, amplify it, and paper over the contradictions until the narrative suits our needs now.

In this way, we repeat history in the ways we write our stories. In "The *Empire* Strikes Back: A Post-Transsexual Manifesto" Sandy Stone argues that writing history is a "struggle to ground an account in natural inevitability." Each historical narrative strives to make "an authoritative and final explanation for the way things are, and consequently for the way they must continue to be." We make the histories we write feel inevitable. And this inevitability creates a waiting period, placing the now somewhere else, somewhere in the future. We can't live otherwise in the present, and we couldn't have lived otherwise in the past. Our stories follow mappable arcs that rarely present different trajectories.

Writing my history in this way requires me to reduce Bessie to her extraordinary gender-defying traits, overlooking other aspects of her life. I must make her the mythic mountain woman of yore. She must be strong and resolute and smart and accomplished. She wasn't a shamed woman; she wasn't dirty, run down, a drudge. She wasn't an illiterate hillbilly—not *that kind* of country woman. But the mythic mountain woman trope is also an incomplete, often purposefully constructed narrative. Bessie died young, and no one alive today knew her or what the rest of her story held, so this transformation isn't too difficult to make. She's an easy archival target.

To make this narrative work, I must also cast off the parts of myself that don't fit the narrative, the parts that existed before I had consciousness of my transness and the language to name it. I must then excavate my stories that mirror hers and evaluate them with theory to make my experiences read as transgender, queer, Appalachian. This allows me to speak from a place of authority both as her ancestor and as a properly transgender and rural person. Then I can achieve a definitive narrative, a plausible history, something that feels inevitable.

My training has made it hard for me to remember how life felt without this theory and its accompanying lingo. I don't know that I had gendered shame from my relatives, or that my shyness was a result. I remember feeling a general confusion at the world. I wasn't out of place in my social environment or the physical landscape. Maybe the disconnect came because I wasn't a very good farm kid. Unlike my cousins, I couldn't do basic farm tasks. I spent too much time inside, and I didn't know how to or want to hunt. I didn't know how to grow food with my hands or how to care for farm animals. I didn't know how to build things. I worked hard, but my work was never correct.

Maybe even this wasn't the case. I had interests outside of the family. My nuclear family was sheltered, evangelical Christians while the rest of the family wasn't. I went to church in a big city and had big-city friends. It could have been that my interests were considered fancy or urban, things that required too much time spent inside alone and not enough family time. Then there's the isolation children suffer when their parents and adult relatives don't get along. There are so many more reasons that could explain why I felt like I didn't entirely fit in, and I don't want this retroactive shame to become the sole story. I don't want to create a dominant narrative at the expense of the more complicated reality to gain the acceptance of legible visibility over authentic representation.

When it comes to Bessie, I have no reason to connect her to my gendered childhood story other than a deep fascination. I can't find a logical beginning to my transness or queerness or Appalachian-ness, and mapping theory backwards onto my childhood feels like I'm erasing it or adding yet another label to it that doesn't fit. To get around writing my history from a place of erasure, I must attend to my shame in the present. This shame is harder to deal with and doesn't lend itself to narratives that read well. I must work through the shame of knowing that my past does not fit into a proper transgender, queer, or even Appalachian narrative, that maybe my queer, trans, Appalachian story starts much later in life and doesn't have any connection to back then. How easy it is to slip into the pull of coincidence, of what I read after the fact aligning with what happened in the past. How easy it is to assign a causal link, a plot, a consequence that build up to make something. How cleverly I can write my childhood into a seminar paper, align theory on the page with my lived history. But I don't want to do that because that's not what I experienced. And that's okay. Maybe all this training and theory doesn't serve me.

Excavating my past experiences, braiding them with similar historical narratives, then adding critical reading of my experience to self-theorize, to perform what some call autoethnography, builds momentum by integrating my story into a larger political narrative. This potential version of my story is easy to write and nice to read because it's familiar. The clever association, the placement of research, the parallels make this version of my story seem as though something deep is happening, something difficult to pull off. My experiences gain meaning, seem worth something to history.

I've lived a completely ordinary life, so much that I don't know how to write a transgender or queer or Appalachian story because I don't feel like I've lived one. The moments I've shared passed by in the slow and unyielding lull of the everyday, so unimportant at the time and recalled now only with intention and effort. They did not stick with me so intensely that I needed to relive them on the page. So using literary techniques to make them into something more than they were feels like a sham.

Nevertheless, in searching for ways to write myself in my stories, maybe I can find power in this ordinariness. I can revisit my memories, wade a while in the feeling, and leave again. I can rest with the possibility of letting my memories fade away or lurk beneath the surface unexamined. I can allow Bessie and my younger self to remain unwieldy, to rest in the silences of archive and memory. Maybe from that place I can write narratives that shift and morph into something a little less certain, ones that stop deploying the I, the we, in service of some mission. I can write us into that position which is nowhere, into something that fails to tell a legible story.

ALL IS HANDILY ARRANGED

On the border of the village at a quiet intersection, we gathered at the old firehouse in the late August heat for my aunt's wake. The old firehouse had been converted into a small community center. Inside, old photos of life in the town hung on the brown wood-paneled walls. Folding tables and chairs filled the main room where the fire trucks once parked. Crockpots and serving dishes for the potluck dinner filled the outdated kitchen and the side tables in the main room. Southern metal, country music, and my aunt's favorite, Cher, played from a karaoke machine in the corner of the room. *Believe* was always in the tape deck of her green '90s convertible Mustang as she'd blast down the winding Ohio country roads.

The location of the old firehouse makes it easy to visit and then escape from without having to go into the village, perfect for awkward family gatherings. My family has had a few reunions and celebrations there since the firehouse was converted into a community center, and I enjoy being with my family. In the year since I had last seen them, however, I had begun to dress affirmatively in public again, and because I didn't want to take focus off my aunt or the family grieving and healing together, I chose to conceal myself at the wake.

I walked straight to the kitchen and planted myself in the corner where I could observe and listen. Sitting near the food meant that most relatives would pass me at some point, which lessened the awkwardness of mingling at the dinner tables in full sight of everyone. In the smaller room, I could manage the scale of my grief, sharing it first with only a few relatives before entering the room with them all.

After we settled in and ate, a few relatives stood to share memories. All who spoke remembered Jeanine as rambunctious, a wild child, free, but deeply kind, loving, loyal, and protective. My uncle David stood to give the eulogy and sermon, which touched on the loss of the closeness the family had once maintained. The family grew up in the countryside of this village on family land. They farmed, tended animals, attended school and 4-H, had families of their own, raising them together where they themselves had been raised. They lived as intertwined as they could. As the generations carried on, however, the closeness the family once held seemed to unwind. They had drifted apart geographically and socially. The family traditions were dying out as younger generations only seemed to interact on the internet, too busy to meet in person as they once had. The family Christmases and summer reunions ceased.

Many of my cousins, like me, moved away after high school and didn't return. The funeral was one of the first times we'd all met in a long time. I loved my family deeply and I too missed the family gatherings, the connection I once felt in that county. I shared my uncle's grief, though I felt the reasons for our growing apart were more complicated than simple lack of interest. I wanted to add my feelings to his, to combine our griefs and paint a more complete portrait of our dissolution.

My older family members seemed not to have much of a plan to live by. They woke up day after day, did their good, hard work and then received an outcome—families, houses, land, retirement, leisure time. In a way, much as they and their ancestors cultivated the land, they planted their lives by the signs.

Planting by the signs was a way of planting crops and vegetables that followed the daily zodiac cycles of the year. During the Moon's twenty-nine-day cycle around the Earth, it passes through the twelve zodiac signs and their constituent four elements. One planted aboveground crops during waxing moons—from new to full—and underground crops on waning moons. During the time of water and earth signs, one planted crops and pruned for growth. During air and fire signs one weeded, tilled, and pruned to control growth. Planting was never done on Sundays, or when the Moon was in a phase change—new, full, or either quarter.

In his 1830 tract *The Complete Explanation of the Calendar, with a Comprehensive Instruction of the Heavenly Bodies,* the Lutheran minister E. L. Walz of Hamburg, Berks County, Pennsylvania wrote that following the celestial order of the universe "brings light and order in all the multitudinous and the innumerable relationships and operations, with which the people of Earth are interconnected." To the Pennsylvania Dutch, the signs supposedly governed their physical, spiritual, and communal existence. At the time, people believed that if one did everything in its proper order, life would eventually work out. Doubters were ordered to try harder and wait for the results to manifest

My great-grandfather William was a tractor mechanic and farmer who raised eleven children. My grandfather retired from a paper pulp plant and my grandmother worked odd jobs but was mostly a housewife. The family members of their generations all had houses, land, children, grandchildren. The time in which they came to adulthood in rural Ohio was drastically different from mine.

The countryside I grew up in was different, and so too was the city that supported it. In his book *Glass House: The 1% Economy and the Shattering of the All-American Town,* the Lancaster-raised author Brian Alexander writes that "until the 1990s, you couldn't spend more than a few days, even a few hours, in Lancaster without somebody trying to indoctrinate you as to why Lancaster was an exceptional town, and why living there was the same kind of lucky break as being born in America." Lancaster was the main source of jobs and the economic driver of the county, where the famous Anchor Hocking glass factories and distribution centers were located as well as Diamond Power, multiple shoe factories, and a historic downtown shopping area with movie theaters, drive-ins, shopping plazas, and large department stores.

During the latter half of the twentieth century, the town remained, as Alexander says, a place where "you could walk off the high school graduation stage on Saturday and walk into a plant on Monday, where you could stay for the next forty years." People could find easy employment in town as electricians, mill workers, mechanics, machine operators, factory workers, garment makers, department store workers, glass blowers, mechanics, shoemakers.

There was also plenty of leisure to be had. There were churches, like the one my family attended for most of their lives, 4-H, FFA, and home economics organizations, county fair activities, local community festivals, and local gardening associations. There were pools, civic groups, country clubs (though these were out of reach for many in my family), the Elks lodge. By all accounts the county prospered, so much that in 1946, Forbes named the county's main city, Lancaster, the "All American Town." The county was a place you wouldn't want or need to move away from. Life in the county embodied the Pennsylvania Dutch saying "Grow your seeds where they're planted." And the generations before me could. Nothing propelled them out of the region.

My family was so content and stable there for so long that I can summon them out of the past in an instant to bring them to life on the page. A newspaper article from 1951 announces the Carroll Community Garden Club October meeting at the Methodist Church social room. The room was decorated for the season, filled with "arrangements of nuts, squash, corn and seed pods, mums and cabbage heads, and a pumpkin." A guest entertainer presented a cornet solo from Franz von Suppé's *Poet and Peasant Overture*, and there was a lecture on "what could still be planted by gardeners" during the season, like bulbs, daffodils, and evergreens. Members brought floral arrangements and held a bulb sale. My great aunts Dolores and Normalene and my grandfather Donnie attended the flower show as well as the wiener roast and game night held just before the club meeting.

Thirty-three years later, a newspaper announcement from 1984 reads, "Golden Wedding Anniversary Set" below a photo of my great-grandparents Beatrice and William–the one that hung over the mantel of my childhood home. The article announces that "the couple's 50th wedding anniversary party was set for Saturday, July 29th with an open house held at the family home, hosted by their 11 children." The paper notes that William was a retired tractor mechanic and farmer, and that Mrs. Grover was still "busy at home-making" after fifty years. How satisfied and bonded my family was at that time.

My parents married the same year as my great-grandparents' fiftieth wedding anniversary, and life at the time still mostly mirrored that of the generations before them. They met in the village, where they attended the same school their parents had. My father got a good job after high school that he never left. He and my mother raised us on family land in the house my grandfather had built, which they eventually bought from him. My father worked hard. He never brought any complaints he may have had home to us. It never seemed like there was some master plan—or perhaps this was the whole plan, and they followed the script, and it worked out. They went to church on Sundays, attended family gatherings, went to the movies, cooked dinner, and raised us. They had a regular, normal, scheduled life. But the rumblings of change had entered the region as they were coming into adulthood not long before my birth.

Walking across the high school graduation stage and straight into a guaranteed job as a way of life was beginning to fade. The 1980s brought Reagan and the rise of Friedman economics, which was characterized by a focus on corporate takeovers and unregulated profit. The government loosened tax regulations and laws governing large corporations. As Brian Alexander writes, the sole focus of long-standing companies in the county like Anchor Hocking became profit rather than "employment, community cohesion, and general welfare of the country."

As a result, the federal budget deficit soared, as did rates of child poverty, food insecurity, crime, and drugs—the symptoms of a vast national recession that affected everyone, including my home county. Downtown businesses that had been open for a century closed. In 1981 Anchor Hocking halved its numbers of employees. In 1987 four other large employers in the county closed. The mall opened the same year, pulling business away from the historic downtown. Property and income tax levies raised to fix the town failed. Schools in the county crumbled.

Socially, the way of life I was born into, the way I thought the world worked and how my future would turn out, wasn't different from that of my predecessors. I felt no pressure or desire to do anything other than live where I had always lived, like everyone around me. I wanted a house, probably the one I'd grown up in, and I wanted to work one job for my entire career, manage the land, and keep a garden, a barn, and some animals. School was just something to do during the day, and I felt no pressure to achieve or to think about college. Neither my parents nor their siblings had attended college, and some of them didn't even graduate high school. The idea of college was present, some invisible force pushing my generation along, so I vaguely planned to go. When my guidance counselor—who graduated from the school with my older relatives—heard that I planned to apply, he simply told me that my family doesn't go to college, that I should find a trade. During my last two years of high school, I attended a career center for culinary arts and worked three jobs. I saved money, spent thriftily, and went to family reunions and lunches and holiday gatherings. I was doing everything right, and I never wanted to leave.

Yet I walked across my high school graduation stage into a recession. School levies failed to pass; the housing boom collapsed after predatory lending law protections were overturned. Housing prices rose, student debt skyrocketed, and the economy shifted to gig work while wages stagnated.

I read the signs, maintained the order, and honored all that my family had taught me. I wasn't sure if the process would ever pay off like it had for them, but through the doubt, I wished for nothing more than the life they had. Yet no matter how much time we spent together living on the same land, in the same houses, attending the same family gatherings, going to the same schools, doing everything as if time had stood still, the county we had all grown up in stopped providing opportunity. There was no longer any real chance to follow the age-old plan that was not a plan.

Life could not turn out for me as it had for older generations of my family, so eventually I moved to the big city to attend school and find work. I scraped by, waiting to be able to afford anything I could call my own, a house or land—a garden, a patch of trees or unobstructed sky, the space in which to gather. I didn't want to be out of step with the seasons, inundated with the noise and movement and speed of the everyday chaos of the metropolis. I didn't want to be stuck in a place so removed from all I'd ever known.

Yet for my generation, moving out of the region was seen as a choice, as if something other than simply needing to earn a living lured us out of the county. Staying was presented as an option, obscuring all the factors that seemed to conspire against our potential to live there. Staying was a long-term fight that we might not win, that might take more from us than we could gain from it, but it was still seen as a viable decision. And I didn't ever want to be away. In the big city I felt as though I was only ever passing the time, waiting to return. I wanted all that I'd had before. I wanted a home.

But at home, winds grew quiet, fields sat fallow. The city school and a new housing development paved over the fields near my house. The county felled trees to extend roads and power lines to accommodate the expansion. The old family houses creaked and moaned in the valleys, shifting, molding, crumbling away. The animals disappeared. The relatives of my generation had to take long flights or car rides to meet back home, we didn't own houses in which to gather, and many of us couldn't take off work to spend time together. So we looked to the internet to stay connected. We messaged and shared with one another, hoping it would be a temporary expedient, hoping we could meet in the old houses on the old land once so accessible to us. The technology that actively aided our continued isolation was the only thing that tethered us together.

When I turned to theory to make sense of my conflicted feelings, trying to reconcile the trans life I was leading in major cities with the way I was raised, I was left wanting. In the cultural theorist Lauren Berlant's book *Cruel Optimism,* I learned that all I wanted to claim in my life—space, land, family, leisure—constituted a "cluster of promises" that I might never achieve. My longing for and striving toward these dreams manifested as an "optimism" that was "cruel" because it was the very thing that kept me from prospering. If I gave up on the pursuit of my dreams, I might free myself from my dissatisfaction.

According to queer theorist Jack Halberstam, these promises constitute the definition of the American Dream, heteronormative standards of success, so there is power in failing to achieve them. He writes that "queerness offers the promise of failure as a way of life . . . but it is up to us whether we choose to make good on that promise in a way that makes a detour around the usual markers of accomplishment and satisfaction."

I tried hard to craft some non-normative way of living in the cities I moved to. I tried to experience my transgender self to the fullest. I finally had hormones and a name that fit me, a body that daily felt more like mine. I had the language to express myself. I developed close ties to other transgender people, a group of queer people that I labeled my community. I placed my trust in my art, in the ambiguity of living without chasing after some ideal. I tried to forget my connection to my heteronormative family, put aside the hope to someday farm or own a house or live in a rural town. I tried to release my ties to all that I cherished.

But removed from the landscape and the people that shaped me, the whole way of life that brought me into being, I couldn't carry on. I couldn't fail in that way, and I didn't want to fail because I didn't want to achieve what mainstream transgender life in the big city laid out for me. I couldn't pit myself against all that my family meant to me to gain acceptance among strangers, to fit—or fail to fit—a script, to gain a label. I didn't want to strive for a way of life that I'd adopted because it wasn't something else. I was tired of clinging to negation.

Sitting in the kitchen at the old firehouse in the village, I wanted to tell David all of this. I wanted to tell him that generational differences were a myth constructed to divide us, that our generation was just as interested in the old ways, that we longed for togetherness and family, that we knew struggle and hardship, but that sometimes no matter how hard we worked, life was just different. All that we wanted might stay forever out of our reach.

I wanted to tell him that I had no real idea how to live as fully and truly as they once had, or how to create a life now or in the future without them. I wanted to share with him that my great-grandparents endeavored to foster a healthy environment based on deep and careful nurturing, and that this careful nurturing allowed all that grew to prosper. I knew that my grandparents and their siblings carried on this endeavor the best they could, but that because of changing circumstances beyond their control, I never had the chance to adapt to the environment in the way they did, to negotiate my terms of living. I couldn't just bloom where I was planted. My generation never really could.

But I didn't say any of this. I sat in silence and listened from the old brown and cream kitchen as the wake carried on and the music shifted to relatives singing karaoke. I was hiding in that kitchen, sad that my aunt had died, fed up with death, with the alcohol and pills and poverty that took so many. Maybe I was too confused to say anything after so much time away from my family. I'd lost the shared language and inflections, the intuitions. I sat silent because I was sick of a twisted temporality that rendered life in the interim between funerals empty. I was tired of saying I was glad to be together no matter the circumstances when circumstances always mattered. And maybe I sat silent in the corner of the kitchen because I wanted to listen and absorb all they had to share. I was still trying to learn my place.

Dead Furrows

Violet's grandmother lies in ashes in a plain porcelain urn on a marble pedestal in the front of the funeral parlor. Violet's aunt bustles around the room double-checking the flowers and the music and the furniture arrangement, ensuring everything is right when nothing about death ever seems right. I offer to help, but Violet's aunt wants the distraction.

We all have our distraction objects. Violet's cousin has errands to run. Violet's grandfather has a last-minute oil change, a carwash. Violet's mother has another load of laundry, already clean floors to scrub.

I have a photograph. Violet's profile photo has changed. Her hair color, too. She sits in front of a castle on a mountaintop in Germany. Her smile carries a sadness underneath, the recognition of autumn's end, when the warmth, color, and fragrant air all give way to cold. Violet has cropped the photo, leaving a small trace of someone's elbow visible beside hers. Violet is particular about how she looks in photographs and wouldn't have cropped one so peculiarly for no reason. She has intentionally removed the person beside her. I know who it is and why she cropped him out, but I don't want to believe it. I can't. To evade the impending weight of the funeral, I focus on the photograph: its story, our story.

Scholars write that evasion is a modern development in the attitude toward death. Until recently, life expectancy was low, mortality was high, and diseases like tuberculosis, diphtheria, pneumonia, and cholera ran rampant. Industrial accidents were prevalent, and childbirth often proved fatal. Most people lived in large extended family networks instead of small nuclear families. Death was a part of life, experienced and cared for in the home by family and friends. Death was so ubiquitous it was built into architecture in the form of death doors—front doors or parlor doors, filled with holes, that could be removed and used to cool corpses.

In writing about death, evasion is similarly built into the architecture of our language. People have passed on, or they're in a better place, gone to the other side, taken their final journey, but they've rarely died. I encounter the same evasion in trying to write about the death of my relationship with Violet. The way I've changed her name because it's too hard to use her real one. The way I've condensed and obscured so many of our moments together so that I can come at them askew and release them little by little back into the narrative to protect myself from their damage.

Violet, whose hair was purple and green when we met. Violet, small limbed, bright, and showy. Violet, who hid her mania in punk music and alcohol, in the shared aggression of the scene, who in the quiet moments was tender and who, when not, made me so desperately want to help transform her. She was a field full of violets, each one different from the next—a field, when all I ever wanted was a garden.

Evasion became the central motif of our relationship. Even now, writing so many years later, I want to paint Violet as the terminally unhappy Lady Brett Ashley, always wanting someplace and someone else. Narrating her into the problem, averting the reality of our situation to create a tidy, acceptable narrative of our hurt is easier than examining it.

Our evasion went back to the beginning. Violet and I met when we were sixteen, during a period when I was hiding in the quiet corners of my small rural world. I spent my days in my room or outside in the wooded hills and creek valley, usually reading. I rarely left home unless it was to follow the creek up the hill to see my cousins or to cross the fields behind our house to my great-aunt's. I went to the mall in the nearest town with my best friend when I could, but I had only been to the big city twice before I met Violet. Violet excited me. She traveled to concerts and house shows and the skatepark. She was constantly moving, and had what to me seemed like an unwavering courage in the face of new experiences I thought I could never manage. I know now that what I saw as excitement was instability, the constant movement for escape. But I wanted to escape; I wanted her to take me somewhere, anywhere. I didn't know then that I'd be trading one set of hiding places for another.

The first time Violet invited me over it was a cold March day, seven years before the funeral. We stood on the sidewalk outside her house under the cheap shade of a petrified birch while she paced and jerked her hands as though engaged in physical combat with all that troubled her. I would come to know these motions well, to see the physicality of her mania and depression, the rage bubbling and spilling out over them.

In that flippant way only a teenager can speak, Violet finally said: *My mom's the worst and probably won't want you to come over. I'm going to go in first. I'll come to get you when you can come in.*

I sat outside, waiting. I knew her mom wasn't the reason she didn't want me to come in. I knew she used her mom, as teens often use their parents, as an excuse. Embarrassed by my home life, I too had made up parental reasons to excuse myself from various activities. It is one of the open secrets of adolescence. As I stood outside, I heard screaming and the breaking of many fragile things, and then the front door swung open, crashing into the porch's support beam. Violet's purple and green hair emerged as her hand rose to catch the door on the backswing. She looked at me and said only: *Come back in an hour.*

I left and walked up the hill to my friend Lux's house. Lux had introduced me to Violet, calling me one night to tell me I'd been set up on a date.

You'll love Violet, she's wild, Lux told me on the phone with that excitement in their voice that made me feel like I could do anything.

Lux and I had dated briefly and remained close friends, so my unexpected arrival was not uncommon or unwelcome. We walked down the steep wooded hill behind their house, an odd choice—there was a paved road we could have walked down—made odder still by Lux's decision to wear an old pair of duct-taped black platform boots. Our destinations were Blockbuster, to rent horror videos, and Avondale's to pick up a pizza. Lux's platform heels collapsed and they stumbled a bit, but we made it home unharmed. We made brownies, and while we waited for them to bake, we fervently debated topics ranging from George W's mixed metaphors to the use of the Oxford comma to gender restrictions in the military to Ben Kingsley's chameleon acting abilities to authors we loved—like Edgar Allan Poe, Agatha Christie, and Emily Dickinson—and how many Shakespeare lines we could quote from memory in our best English accents.

In between the movies, I called Violet's house periodically for the next four hours to see if my hour of waiting had ended, but she never answered. Eventually, Lux and I fell asleep in a pile of blankets, black clothes, and platform boots, our faces and hair stuck with the brownie remnants of a small but fierce food fight, the Halloween string lights on the porch casting orange over the spent pizza box and crinkled soda cans as the sounds of the Dresden Dolls, the Cure, or Tori Amos played in the background. I can only guess at the music, but what is embedded in my memory was that the first time I visited Violet's house, I was somewhere else with someone else who treated me the way I so desperately hoped she would.

If evasion was our central motif, denial was our theme. I told Violet that I was transgender when we met. I hoped that by spending as much time as possible in town with her I would see other transgender teens in the privacy of the park or at weekend basement parties while parents were away. I didn't know the depths of her bipolar disorder, the gravity of it, or the severity of her substance abuse, already in place by sixteen. I couldn't see then how these would worsen or the ways I would become buried under the weight of them.

The denial came subtly at first, in the way that things are subtle when one doesn't have a frame of reference to understand them as warnings. In the beginning, I don't think her actions were intentional. She just did them, and through repetition they formed feedback loops that taught her how to shield herself and others from what she was feeling.

The troubling signs seeped in little by little after I moved in with Violet about a year after we started dating like when I'd ask her for advice on outfits or makeup. She would help at first, then refuse. *It's not my job to help you be a woman. You wanted this—you do it.*

I felt guilty asking her for help, for burdening her with my failed femininity. I had not learned to be a girl quietly and invisibly. I didn't know at the time that femininity is learned and practiced, or that drawing attention to the learning process could cause such strife. I came to understand that learning femininity would be solely my burden to carry.

I began testing dresses in public when I was with her. Once we went to a concert and I wore green and black striped tights under a black miniskirt, black six-inch platform boots, and a Bauhaus T-shirt. I felt a freedom I hadn't before. I walked around the venue noticing silent nods and approving smiles. We ran into some of Violet's friends. I stood silent as they exchanged pleasantries, but her mood changed after that interaction.

You look stupid. You should take that off.
Are you sure? I thought I looked okay but . . .
You should go change.

I had brought a change of clothes with me—a practice I still use when I go to unfamiliar places—in case I got too overwhelmed to wear a skirt and for the walk in and out of the house. I thought

I looked pretty, but I trusted Violet's expertise, expertise I mistakenly thought I didn't hold. I just wanted to have a good time at the concert, and baggy clothes could so easily hide all my hurt. At least I could disappear into the crowd and focus on the music. I wanted to do better, to become a better girl. I most certainly did not want to look bad.

I imagine now that some part of Violet's mind backed away from the prospect of conflict arising with her friends about my being transgender, even though one never manifested. I imagine her mind built up reasons to rid herself of the possibility before the experience occurred. I had done the same by trying to shield my friends from her bipolar. I know she didn't think she could uplift me in that moment, just as I couldn't uplift her. Because I couldn't uplift myself.

I tried talking to Violet about what I was experiencing, hoping I could help her understand, hoping that if I could just explain my gender to her, I could explain it to myself. Her responses were variations of the same theme:

Can we talk about something else?

I don't know what you expected? You wanted this.

I don't want to spend all our time together talking about you being miserable because you want to wear dresses.

Year after year, while I attempted to understand myself, Violet's substance abuse increased. She was often drunk, which I mostly wrote off as simply a feature of the alternative scenes we took part in. I never tried alcohol as a teen, but the other teens around me drank casually and I found it an exciting change of pace from my normal quiet life. When Violet finally saw a doctor for bipolar medication about a year after we met, I was hopeful that she would want to medicate less with alcohol, but she abused the medication too. She wouldn't take it regularly, and then when she did, she'd take a handful of Xanax and have three-day blackouts, during which

I'd care for her. Entire events—concerts, friends' birthdays, family gatherings—would be lost in the haze. I'd explain away her drunkenness or her Xanax sedation as a fickle stomach, a bad day, a spell.

One night at a party where she'd been drinking, she had sex with her friend. She apologized, promising to stop drinking and abusing Xanax. And for a time she did, and for a time I wanted to give her all my support, so ready to help ease the burdens hiding the person inside, the person I wanted despite all the mess. I didn't know how to uphold boundaries, understand that I was not the appropriate person to help her, or realize that I could have asked for help. Teens often accept the strangeness of their lives and navigate what they're given the best they can, together. I couldn't see how my actions, this readiness to help and to forgive, would only perpetuate the negative behavior.

And just as things seemed to be getting better, they got so much worse. Violet began sleeping around with girls she knew, and this time, not under the influence of alcohol or Xanax. *It doesn't count; they're girls.*

I heard this refrain so often I'd find myself repeating it every time she cheated, again and again, as if it were a prayer that would console me. I came to believe I was denying her, denying her sexuality, while I concentrated so much on wanting mine to be validated. The thought suffocated and silenced me. I stopped questioning her; I stopped talking about it. Violet never directly said that I wasn't a girl, but the girls she slept with were girls, and she needed to sleep with them, and I wasn't like them, my body was not like theirs. My dysphoria intensified. I was caught between not being able to be a girl and not being a good enough boy to be desired.

At that time, the sex we did have turned increasingly aggressive and particularly gendered. She wanted me to take the role of a dominant, insensitive man. *I want you in control. Fuck me like I don't mean anything.*

I didn't want to play a role that betrayed who I was. I told her I wanted her in the same way she wanted other girls. But she was insistent, as if sex were a ritual that through repeated action would transform me into the kind of boy she wanted.

For a few years, Violet was never physically violent with me. Her outbursts, her mania, her depression led to fighting, to screaming, to what I now know was emotional abuse. Then she started slapping me, pushing me, throwing anything she could find: a candle, a plate, a coffee mug, a plaster crucifix her grandmother had made.

I never defended myself. I tried to hide from her physical outbursts, to quickly appease her to end the chaos. I never worried about injury and I never wanted to hurt her back. Violet was small, under five feet tall, while I was over six. I was physically bigger than her and I knew she was hurting under all the rage. More than that, I was not read as a woman, and if in the process of defending myself she received an injury, I didn't want to face the consequences of so many men, read as a domestic violence perpetrator. The thought of men's jail, of all the ways that my body—my gender and the misreading of it—could be used as a weapon against me, made the situation impossible to navigate. I was stunned into inaction. At worst I just bore the duration of her outbursts, and at best I played caretaker after they subsided.

I tried to discuss with Violet how her actions hurt me. When she was depressed, bringing up these problems would send her spiraling into further darkness, into saying things that reversed the gravitational pull of the conversation and left me apologizing to her.

When she was in a state of days- or weeks-long mania, the rapidness of her actions and her constant transformations were disorienting. She'd deflect all criticism during those times. Her responses lacked all recognition of culpability:

But I'm productive now.
I'm not angry or depressed.

None of that before was me, not really—this is me now.
Do you want to take my happiness away from me?
Can't you just celebrate this with me?

Her responses silenced me. My dysphoria darkened and took shape around me. I let it shroud my concerns; my girlhood became a dusty dresser in a forbidden room. After so many years together I didn't know what else to do. I couldn't stand to look back and think that the years weren't worth it. I must just hide my hurt and move on.

As a defense, I hid my friends and family away. I tried to create distance between them and Violet in the hopes that distance with them was an easier battle than the one I fought with her, that one day we could find our ways back together, that friendships would not end. I did this to hide them from her rage. I did this to hide them from my shame.

Just as I hid Violet from my family, she denied our problems to hers. When her family eventually asked for photos of us, she would send ones showing the rare moments when we were both smiling, both happy and forgetting—or hiding—our history for a moment. The one we took at Christmas at my great-aunt's, an event Violet had prepared for by taking her medication properly for weeks before; the one of us on vacation on Mount Washington in Pittsburgh, where none of the ties that bound us mattered, and so she was freed. These photos that lined up on her grandmother's mantel narrated a fantasy. This fantasy was one of the few places where our narratives mirrored one another. For seven years, both of us constructed a world in which things weren't as bad as they seemed.

During our seven years together, we sometimes lived together, sometimes apart. Violet spent the year before the funeral in Germany, and before that multiple semesters and summers there. She went to college in Michigan, where we lived together for a year before I moved back into her house. We lived apart for three years, and upon her return, my only chance to see her for a while, she wanted to spend her free time in Michigan seeing her friends. *I have so much studying to do while I'm here. You can't blame me for studying. You'll be a distraction.*

I had just finished a semester driving between my campus in Ohio and three jobs in two cities. Most weekends when I got off work I'd drive the two hundred miles between Ohio and Michigan to see her. I'd stay a day, rising early on Sunday to do my homework while she was asleep, then finishing it later during the drive back, in gas station parking lots and diners dotting the interstate. In the previous two years, I had put one hundred thousand miles on my car traversing the Midwest landscape to see her. Three jobs and a full course load didn't distract me from her.

Violet returned from Germany two months before the funeral, then left again to begin a master's program. During those months she had been avoiding me, and the gap between us grew wider. We had dinner together maybe twice.

I have so many friends to see while I'm here. I want to make sure I see them first. You understand, right?

I understand.

I didn't recognize it then, but I realize now we were both creating barriers to justify and insulate our feelings, to avoid blame. I was building up the narrative that I was the dutiful partner, the one trying. She was building up the narrative that I was the problem, that I was clingy, distracting, didn't take her schooling seriously. I put in so much effort to divert myself from the heart of the matter, so much effort doubling down on my own pain that I didn't know other narratives were open to me. I could never see those choices hiding behind the pain, never work out how to move beyond the catastrophic endings I thought lay there. I didn't think I could walk away.

I walk outside the funeral home into the relentless August heat and watch the cars pass. Violet calls me. *How's it going? I'm busy right now so I don't have much time and I'm almost out of credits to call you.*

Everyone is holding up. We're busy getting ready. I'm glad you called. I love you.

I love you. The words come out of my mouth as a reflex, a last-ditch defense to convince myself everything is okay. *Everyone is holding up.* I am holding up. She doesn't say it back. I can hear the person beside her, the person cropped out of her photos. I imagine she is hiding me from him too, the mysterious him who only has a first name, a friend she's only just met. I lie. I'm not holding up. I've taken time off work and school to be here. I shouldn't have stretched myself to this point. I don't want to play her archimime, her surrogate griever.

Cars pull into the parking lot, arranged in rows of three as the funeral home staff waves them in with orange flags the reflective color of hunting hats. The cars look like cattle coming back to the barn—slow, unwieldy, finding it difficult to navigate the confined space.

Violet's family is Catholic, so I feel awkward being around them. I don't know how to perform the rituals. I've been given a rosary, but I don't know what to do with it, so it hangs on my arm, a shameful beacon I feel offends the relatives who pass by me. I know the otherness I feel can only be amplified by the way I look. I feel like her family sees me as the boy who corrupts their precious girl, a deviant, long-haired misfit. I am not the woman their precious girl hides from them. My grief is invisible. I swallow it.

The usher puts a hand on my shoulder and guides me into the funeral home. I walk down the hallway past the main doorway to the second entrance at the front. I want to slip in without having to run the gauntlet of properly wielded rosaries.

The priest opens the memorial service with a prayer, followed by a brief hymn. Then the procession of eulogies begins. Violet's relatives speak—her aunt, her mother, her grandfather, who recounts his fifty-three-year relationship with his wife. I stare at a stain in the carpet that's been torn to fit the podium, losing focus on the surrounding space. The stain pulsates, expands, and contracts, lightens and darkens, changes color. I hear my name and look up to see Violet's grandfather pointing to me. —*like the relationship they have. It's precious, worth protecting at all costs. Hold onto that love and love fiercely. Don't let it go. Not for anything.*

I nod and turn away to stare at the stain on the carpet. It seems to have grown since I last looked at it, morphing into various shapes. It takes the shape of my hidden womanhood. It takes the shape of the relationship Violet's family thinks we have. It takes the shape of her. I hide my face. I don't want to let them see me not crying. I don't want to let them see me unmoved by death.

The service continues and I leave to find a quiet corner in the parlor. The parlor is my favorite part of the funeral home, the room that holds the coffee. I've gravitated here during memorial services throughout my life: my great-grandmother's, grandmother's, great-uncle's, great-aunt's, my best friend's roommate's. The first time I was in this room I was more than a foot shorter than I am now, with bright blond hair in a bowl cut with the undersides shaved in the quintessential '90s haircut. I would have been in a suit, an awful constrictive thing, and it would have been too big on me. Even then I'd have gotten a cup of coffee—my love affair with it began when I was eight—and sat on the same antique chaise longue in this same room staring at the same generic 1970s wall art. Here in the corner is another stain in the carpet—one I made when I was eleven. I know I won't look suspicious if I sit alone next to the coffee. The machine gives me a convenient excuse, a friend pulling me away from an awkward social encounter. I stare at the stain I made, then deep into the darkness of my coffee.

Inside the hospice center two days before the funeral, the quiet shuffle of the death vigil has begun. Violet's grandmother lies dying in a bed and I'm alone with Violet's family. Her grandmother didn't want Violet to disrupt her studies to come home from Germany since she had just visited two weeks ago, before her grandmother was diagnosed, before anyone knew she was sick. The tumors grew so rapidly in her lungs that Violet's grandmother hadn't even gone to a doctor, thinking she just had congestion or chest pain, some affliction she could walk off.

Earlier in the afternoon, I walked off the cement pathways of the neatly manicured lawn into the woods behind the hospice center to be alone. The hospice center is nestled flat in the valley between Black Hand sandstone cliffs, the highest peaks of which jut hundreds of feet above the ground. In the shade, the hot autumn air cools as it dips into the valley of Pleasant Run where it flows behind the hospice center. Water spiders snap across the surface, muddy from rains. Blue jays, chimney swifts, and eastern phoebes flit from branch to branch, plunging toward the water before darting into the narrow lick of blue sky. Unlike many of the streams in Appalachia, Pleasant Run is free of acid mine drainage. I stick my hand in, feel its force, its age, the layers of stone carved by its ceaseless flowing, the connection of this small region to others.

I came to the water's edge to escape the hushed voices, the hushed eating, the hushed food. The absurdity of mourning food, flavorless subsistence food: pale cornbread, anemic potatoes, strips of dry chicken, as if no taste exists in grief, as if savoring while mourning equates to savoring death. Maybe people do eat their feelings, so mourners need this, but the food feels thoughtless, so out of touch with the comfort I've experienced eating with my family after loss. Maybe my distance to the people in the room, the knowledge that the food wasn't prepared for me, renders it inedible. Violet's family remains a mystery, even after seven years, a map I was given without a key. The mutual unknowing hovered between us in that silent room, a fogged gorge, a crumbling bridge. I hold the mossy sandstone, the water's pulse, as I drift above that bridge, out of the fog, into the sky, morphing into a single buzzing shape, the shimmering underbelly of silver maples.

Sitting beside Pleasant Run that day, I wanted an explanation for why I was at the hospice center, but I never found one, and I have blank spots in the timeline where I found the experiences too hard to hold. I want to fill in the gaps, temper the memories, imbue them with a sense of order and meaning. For assistance I turn to the archive, to the technical prose of nineteenth- and twentieth-century accounts of death and dying in central Appalachia. The logic and orderly progression of these old accounts comfort me. I hope to borrow some of the surety of their functionalism to explain my peculiar teleology.

Historically in Appalachia, communities provided food to allow the family to keep watch over their dying loved one. During this death vigil or "sitting up," extended family, neighbors, and fellow churchgoers would bring food, coffee, and tea to the mourning family. In his memoir *Brother to a Dragonfly*, civil rights activist and Baptist preacher Will David Campbell wrote, "Somehow, in rural Southern culture, food is always the first thought of neighbors when there is trouble." The provision of food lifts a burden from the grieving family.

The death vigil most commonly practiced in Appalachia dates to medieval and Renaissance Europe, when a continuous watch was held at the bedside of the dying until they passed, and subsequently until other mourners had a chance to visit. Some vigils were large affairs; others were only for those invited by the family. The vigil could last months, weeks, days, or hours, depending on how long death took to arrive.

The deathwatch purportedly served many functions, allowing time for family members and neighbors to help cook, perform household chores, and tend to children, animals, and crops. Visitors came to assuage the loneliness of the grieving family, to show respect, to bid farewell. Esther Sanderson in *Scott County and Its Mountain Folk* explained that in Appalachia, it was an unthinkable social taboo to not show up for the deathwatch, even if long travel was required.

There was a physical practicality to the deathwatch. Houses had to be heated or cooled and bodies, before and after death, needed constant care. In a process called "laying out," which was conducted before rigor mortis—commonly called "cold death" or "stiffening"—set in, the body was placed on a cooling board, which was sometimes just a plain wooden board covered in a sheet or a door taken off its hinges. The corpse was bathed, the face and extremities washed with lye soap and water or a cloth dipped in soda water, camphor, and vinegar or alcohol to prevent discoloration. The hair was combed and the face shaved if needed. A cloth was tied around the head and under the chin to keep the mouth from falling open. If the eyes were not closed before rigor, weights, usually coins, would be placed on the eyelids to give the corpse the appearance of sleep. In warm weather, mourners would fan the corpse to keep it cool. The overnight watch was necessary to protect the corpse from flies, rats, and cats.

The death vigil served an important social function. Attending a deathwatch was a way to be seen, to begin the cycle of reciprocity so that when the day came, the community would return the favor. The death vigil was also a spectacle, an event to be witnessed and later recounted to others. In "The Death and Burial of Boney Bill Scalf," Henry Scalf writes, "Cousin Ruth walked back and forth through the house, telling all who came: 'I held his hands for him when he was dying. He wanted it that way.'"

Attitudes toward death have changed since the nineteenth century. Sickness and death have largely been hidden away in medical facilities, the act of care transferred from family and friends to trained medical staff. The home is no longer the most common domain of death. Furthermore, technologies such as temperature-controlled rooms and embalming have slowed the process of decomposition and kept scavengers away. Mourners are now mostly absent from the process of corpse care. The immediate family is thus freed to handle domestic affairs. For the most part, friends and community members now visit after death at the showing or the funeral, or they simply send condolences. Now social proximity dictates whether friends and community members should attend to the bereaved, whether their presence will burden the family. The taboo has shifted from not being in the proper place to not knowing it.

Violet's aunt texts me to come back inside the hospice center. I walk past the garden, wet with bloom, to the sliding glass door of Violet's grandmother's room and look through the window. The family huddles around a tiny pale body with hair wispy as an acanthus bush left to grow unnoticed. I step inside and Violet's aunt takes my hand.

The priest performs last rites at her bedside and the family responds in unison to the prayer. As Violet's grandmother starts to slip away, the family begins to sing "Amazing Grace." I grew up the child of a pastor in an evangelical church, an upbringing that taught me how to function in awkward situations and the words to dozens of hymns that people sing during them. I listen as the passages stucco with choked diaphragms, dry mouths, spongy, salted tears. I mouth the words I've mouthed a thousand times in church:

> Through many dangers, toils, and snares,
> I have already come
> 'Tis grace hath brought me safe thus far,
> And grace will lead me home.

No part of this moment feels like grace for Violet's grandmother or for her family. Mercy maybe, but not grace. No elegance rests in the room, no honor or refinement fills its stillness. Grace could be the goodwill we offer her, the way I play the good neighbor. But there's no grace in it for me either. I want more out of this moment, more out of the separation of death, not this ceasing, this stasis where nothing moves on, nothing moves, nothing moves me. I want the grace of the song to rid me of my shame. I want to leave but I'm held in place by hands pulling tighter as I try to move away from death unfolding in front of me.

The family trails off into silence when the doctor shakes his head in a gesture of certainty. Violet's aunt releases my hand, wipes her nose, and stifles her sobs as she arranges the flowers on the stand beside her mother with exactitude. The family members wipe their faces, straighten their clothes, and line up beside the bed to prepare for the traditional photo with the deceased sitting up in bed. I know this tradition; I've seen pictures of older family members standing around the deathbeds of my ancestors. I try looking anywhere but at Violet's grandmother or her family. I close my eyes, conjuring the photo albums that line the top of my grandmother's old closet and try so desperately to transport myself into a photograph of the family in which I belong—a birthday party, sitting around my grandmother's all-white Christmas tree, behind the barn with my grandfather, in a tree with my cousin, at my grandmother's funeral. I am a ghost in the corner of the hospice room, flickering, captured before I can fade away.

Traditionally in Appalachia, the records describe, the mourning family decided how to arrange the corpse and room based on the specifics of the death culture in which they took part. The positioning of the corpse was vital. The legs were extended, the arms folded, the hands placed on top of the chest, the head and face held in place by pillows to keep it facing forward. These standards, however, were not universal. The gender, age, and status of the corpse translated to different bodily ideals and thus different body positions. Postures were similarly manipulated to give the illusion of sleep in order to ensure rest for the dead. Objects were used to enhance the positioning of the corpse. Sometimes the intent was to obscure it or to hide it altogether—for example, by covering the body with a blanket, placing flowers on it, or shrouding it.

The laying out of the corpse was accompanied by elaborate ritual practices and performances. In parts of Appalachia, traditional corpse decorations included personal effects, toys, shells, rocks, and pottery sherds. Weeds, wildflowers, crepe paper flowers, and homemade wreaths gradually gained popularity as a form of decoration in the United States after the mid-nineteenth century.

Artists commonly portrayed the dead in watercolor paintings distributed to the mourning families. When photography came to Appalachia, some adopted it as a method to capture the memory of loved ones. Feelings about photography at the time were mixed. Some in the region were superstitious about it; others found it entirely mundane.

Photographs were taken in a variety of settings: inside the house, outside in a yard or field, at the grave before burial. Photographers were hard to come by in the nineteenth and early twentieth centuries, so photos were rarely taken while the person was alive. In this regard, photographs also furnished evidence the person was dead and served as a memento mori, a way to remember the dead and help in the grieving process. Some photographs were kept by family members while others adorned tombstones.

Our understanding and experience of death affects how we view the corpses we encounter. If our experiences with corpses are few, they seem alien, disturbing, unnatural. Conversely, if the normal rituals of daily life include corpses—living bodies in contact with dead ones—encountering bodies becomes mundane.

I never got to know Violet's grandmother, so the corpse I encounter in the hospice center feels only distant and cold. Her body position signals only death.

I hear the clicks, the shifting, the adjustments in the room around me as I try to keep myself in my grandmother's photo albums, safe in a plastic refuge. But someone nudges me to open my eyes for the photo. I look out from my interior photographs to the reality in front of me, the creation of a photo I don't want to see, a photo I won't forget.

In a hospice center on the banks of a quiet creek muddy from rain, a dead woman sits up in bed, surrounded by her family. A ghost hovers in the corner next to them. The lens focuses, the shutter clicks, but no one smiles—they are sentinels guarding the dead and the memories of the living.

I read that after so many vigils, mourners in nineteenth-century Appalachia saw patterns, signs that foretold of death. The three most common were premonitions, visions, and the death rattle. The premonition, the precognition, the forewarning of the end, could be a natural sign, a feeling, or a supernatural experience. A bird flying through an open window or dreams involving the color white were common premonitions of death. Premonition was a gift meant to help one prepare for one's death. Visions before death could be of one's life flashing before one's eyes, a dead family member, or religious figures. The death rattle, a sound emitted by the dying caused by the expulsion of breath through mucus, was the clearest indicator that death was imminent.

I search back through my relationship with Violet for the signs, but no matter how I try, I can't find three singular moments in a series of moments, no major ruptures to signal the end. No premonition of how dark things would get between us, no flash of my life to this point. No death rattle, no hit hard enough, no bruise dark enough, to spur me to fight through the calamity of separation. No gasping for breath, the final *please* from deep down in the chest. Abuse is subtler, less defined, a gradual decline in treatment so the next bad step doesn't seem so bad, until everything is so bad the memory of ever being treated better fades away.

But the signs were all there, ones so easy to recall now that I can go around the wheel chart of transgender and bipolar intimate partner violence and check them off one by one. I can see the isolation, denying my gender and sexuality, using them against me, refusing to talk about them, disapproving of talking to friends about them. The medication abuse, the physical and emotional abuse, denying all culpability during mania, using bipolar disorder to guilt me into forgiving the behavior. When the elements are placed out together in front of me, the list stings with an embarrassing obviousness. But before the funeral, I didn't know what the signs meant or how to read them.

The uncanniness of the vigil stirred me. A rift opened where I had been stuck in the lifeless space between Violet's absence and her grandmother's death. Everything began to look different. Signs became interpretable as something tangible. Again, I wondered why I was at the funeral, why everything ended up this way, where my trajectory lines intersected, what points I could flag and pin so that I could find the wrong turn. I was stuck in what felt like a cruel destiny.

I realize there is no functionalism to explain my situation, no traditions buried in the archive that can neatly and logically order my experiences, no metaphor contained in the language to wrap around the pain and tidy up the mess. No matter how deeply I look, the archive and the metaphors I hoped to find there won't support what I want. I can't answer why I went through what I went through, only describe the way I ended up there.

In the files, I encounter a story I remember from school about a man named William Green. William journeyed from Wheeling, West Virginia to Lancaster, Ohio to build a cabin and raise crops before bringing his family to their new home. The log cabin he wanted to build would have been a simple structure filled with simple furniture. Puncheon benches, stools, or blocks of wood for the tables and chairs, a small kettle or two functioning as a bucket, boiler, and oven. The cabin might have contained a few plates, silverware, a sugar trough for infant beds, and a spinning wheel—items packed on horseback and carried through the wilderness. The food William would have subsisted on has since grown into the heart of midwestern cuisine: cornbread, potatoes, milk, butter, deer, rabbit, turkey, pheasant, squirrel. Early settlers loved pone and johnnycake. Walnut, wild cherry, pawpaw, and plum grew in forests with oak, sugar tree, ash, and buckeye. But William wouldn't build the log cabin; he wouldn't subsist on this food. He fell ill and died shortly after arriving. He was buried in a plain hickory bark coffin on the west bank of Fetters Run, a few yards north of Zanesville Road, east of Lancaster. He left his family in one place and his body in another.

William's story resonates deep within me. Not the surface tragedy, the grand narrative of white colonial settlers pushing west to settle the land, the collective striving, triumph, and tragedy they faced. His story holds a mirror to the sadness and shame I have buried under so many narratives. William's story confirms the emptiness of my search for meaning in tradition. William was not a victim of circumstance. He did not have to leave Europe or leave his family to die far away from home. Nothing changes that fact, no matter how much his circumstances may have felt inevitable, preordained, no matter how much I remember being told that the early white settlers like him were just going with the times, according to their beliefs, that had I been there I wouldn't have thought differently. I too would have simply followed my destiny. After all, even in their deepest tragedies and deaths the early white colonial settlers helped build all we now have. But I know William had a choice.

I know William had a choice because deep down I know that I had one. I felt split between two worlds: the one I denied to be with Violet and the one I thought I was trapped in. I wish I could see the trajectory lines of our relationship, but I know there wasn't a wrong turn.

The truth is that I should have stayed away. I buried the regret and shame of staying with Violet, piling more narratives over it so that digging myself out was not an option, a self-sabotage I used to justify and reinforce my commitment to stay. This narrative heap obscured the knowledge that I shouldn't have separated from family and friends, I shouldn't have given up so much of myself, I shouldn't have seen my path as inevitable, preordained, a tragic fate destined to unfold. I could have stood up for myself. I could have left. I could have and didn't—and that knowledge hurt so much worse than the pretense of my performance at the funeral. I justified my inaction. I made myself the object of my history and not its subject.

Are you ready? Violet's aunt waves to me to come to the car after the funeral mass, the day after the visitation at the funeral home. I don't remember much of the service besides the beautiful organ music and the repetitive standing and kneeling. I know there was an ancient progression to the mass that was followed by congregants reciting from a ritual book. I remember people took part in Communion and brought condolence gifts. I know I sat in the back of the sanctuary with the other non-Catholics and stared at the floor until the service ended.

Since there is no coffin, there are no pallbearers, no procession outside the funeral home, only a small black town car to carry Violet's grandmother's urn to the cemetery.

The cemetery sits low from the road and rises in a dramatic arch through rolling hills that end in a swath of forest. Violet's grandmother's plot sits in the back of the cemetery a few yards from the tree line. The priest transports the cremation urn from the hearse to a small stand in front of her headstone. The priest begins the Rite of Committal—long, unfamiliar, sonorous. The herd of people surrounding the headstone seems restless. Some whisper quietly throughout the service, others shift from one leg to another, lean on their canes. I try to focus on the words I know, but my attention wanders to the old headstones and their engravings. I imagine a time when the symbols and engravings on headstones were common knowledge.

Common grave markers used by early white settlers in Appalachia were wooden crosses and crude slabs of stone with minimal inscriptions. Fieldstones were more lasting than wooden crosses and were often made from various stones and placed on the ground. Decorative markers were also popular. Stonemasons carved symbols, inscriptions, and statues into headstones. Popular symbols, religious and not, included crossbones, death masks, cherubs, hourglasses, clasped hands, a finger pointing toward heaven, a harp or lyre with a broken string, weeping willows, Father Time with a scythe, an open Bible, angels, candles, and lambs.

Flowers and wreaths became popular at funerals in the middle of the eighteenth century and were originally hung on doors as a signal to the community that death had occurred. Families gathered flowers from fields to tie into simple ribbons or cloths to be kept as mementos or sewn into pillows, quilts, or needlework. Weed flowers and dandelions were popular choices. Eventually lilies, daisies, wild roses, apples, and peach blossoms, all symbolizing purity, became popular funerary choices.

In central Appalachia, families and their communities made funeral decorations from what grew locally. Strawflowers, okra pods, milkweed, pussy willows, thistles, cattails, and baby's breath were mixed with greenery like laurel, rhododendron, pine, balsam, fern, hemlock, and boxwood and formed into bouquets and wreaths. Berries, nuts, and crepe paper flowers could be added for decoration. In winter, wreaths were made of holly and cedar, evergreens, and ivy. When funerals became arranged and carried out by professionals, floral arrangements turned to silk flowers, which were cheap to make and buy and offered longevity.

I look at the floral arrangements and the wreaths surrounding Violet's grandmother's simple stone, all bought at the old floral store in town, personalized only by color and the addition of photographs. No symbols or carvings adorn her in-ground stone. It rests as unfamiliar and impersonal to me as her corpse in the hospice center.

The priest lowers and locks the cremation urn into the headstone while saying his final prayers. The crowd disperses. I walk up the hill into the woods behind Violet's grandmother's headstone. During the last few days I have been splitting from myself, seeing myself from outside, how absurd I look standing at the deathbed, the funeral, the gravesite. I see how absurd I look staying in the relationship. I see my friends and family standing around my grave, distant, attending only out of some obligation, a sense of neighborliness, or confusion, not really knowing me, questioning their attendance. I don't want that to be the end of my story.

The truth is that I don't think I ever wanted to be with Violet. I wanted to want her, and I carried shame for not wanting her. I wanted to fix the bad parts of her and, in ways my dysphoria would not let me see, I know I also wanted to be her. Maybe I hoped she'd fix me, that if she could just be more like me, maybe we could be magically transformed into better versions of ourselves. I could finally be a girl, and she could be someone who would want a girl like me. I close my eyes and breathe deep. The rustling of trees and the wind coming over the high hill drown out all sound until it's just me and the earth and it all fades away into one breath, one moment of clarity.

My phone rests on the dinner table after the funeral service. I sit at the emptiest table. I know someone purchased the tablecloths, all red vinyl, from the dollar store. I've bought them in a pinch many times and it seems someone thought to do the same.

Violet posted a photo of her grandfather, mother, aunt, and me standing together at the service, but she cropped me out, leaving only a small portion of my elbow visible.

That's a nice picture. Did you take it? A woman wearing a fake pearl necklace and doused in White Diamonds perfume leans in close, her toxic aroma cloud enveloping me.

Oh, yes, I'm taking some to send to Violet since she's not here.

It's nice that she has such a great friend. Those phones can do so much these days.

The woman excuses herself to go to the restroom while I push a slice of store-bought cake around on my plate. The mourners shuffle in bureaucratic lines around the tables mouthing empty greetings to one another: the ticket line of purgatory.

Fake pearl woman must have powdered her nose with White Diamonds. The scent follows her like a shadow as she creeps across the dirty linoleum back to her seat. I wait until after she sits but just before she settles her cane beside her to take my leave.

Excuse me. I'm going to get some air.

Oh, you must be so tired, young man. Please go.

My fingers tighten around the brown metal folding chair until my hand resembles a crumpled map, blue lines cutting across a ball of bleached paper. I force a smile, throw my cake away, and pour a cup of coffee before walking outside behind the church.

Young man. Violet's mother asked me to look professional, which translates to: don't wear a dress, don't wear makeup, and pull your hair back. I am a stand-in mourner for Violet, a poor replica fooling no one. I can't fool them if they can't see me. The asphalt behind the building morphs into a tightrope, a distraction from the dinner, from constantly being called *him, young man, sir*. I walk around the edges, careful not to touch the grass, and back to the brick wall over and over. The woods at the cemetery created a peace like the one I had in the forest and hillside behind my house, the one I gave up to be with Violet. I want to return to it. I don't want this separation any longer. I know leaving the dinner will cause questions and phone calls, but I can't handle another moment of the farce. I let the cup fall into the grass. I leave.

Violet's ancestors built her house sometime in the 1800s, but half of it burned down in the 1950s and it was remodeled in the 1980s. Now the house, just one floor with blue shutters, looks indistinct, unfinished. Inside the front doorway, a staircase leads nowhere, the only hint of the house's former size. The living room is a cube of wood paneling and brown shag carpet, filled with one blue and white couch, a matching recliner, one end table. Empty bookshelves line the wall. No flowerpots hang from the ceiling and no artwork adorns the walls.

Violet's bedroom—my bedroom—stands just inside the front door. The room is sparse, containing only a small television on a stand, two small bookshelves, and a bed. I close the door and the curtains and turn on the television to whatever channel last played, and plop onto the bed, constricting dress clothes still on. I untie my hair, shake it loose until it spreads wild as acanthus over my pillow. The darkness settles, taking shape around the edges of me, spilling over onto the floor. The light from the television cuts through in small streaks, then forms one large amorphous glow, the light fading away behind enclosing rain clouds. Lying in bed, I lose count of the episodes that play on the television, though my body tells me that night has enveloped the curtained windows. I get up, go to the closet, and change out of my suit into a bra, tight shirt, and miniskirt. I heat up beige food in the beige microwave and return to bed.

The half light of the bedroom casts shadows that soothe my bodily unease. I lie in them and let the force of the day—of every day of the last seven years—come to rest with me. I let the performance end. I didn't know that woman in death or in life. I don't know the woman I am either. The tangled branches of Violet's absence covered any path I may have used to know either. Those branches cover the ground in the garden of my memory. I let my mind wander the twisting passages, the hidden spaces. One corner holds the family celebrations I missed—graduations, weddings, birthdays. The nights spent watching movies and laughing with my brother reside in another. One passageway contains my writing, all the words I hid in a folder on the underside of a dresser drawer or deep within folders within folders on my computer, to hide them from Violet. The passageways are littered with the skirts I hid underneath pants, dresses I wore *just for Halloween*, the moments of seven years of my life recorded in photographs I won't get to keep.

Even if I leave these paths unexplored, I cannot escape all I've hidden from. When I open my eyes, I see them around me. The bedroom is a mausoleum of dusty decorations, placeholders of memory. There is a Campbell's soup wrapper from the first time I came over and Violet made me food—I ate it all and asked for more, even though it was burned and I wanted to go home because something just didn't feel right. There's an envelope of tickets from movies and shows we never attended. There's the broken candle she threw at my head during a petty disagreement that I glued back together and placed in the room as a reminder that broken things can be pieced back together. I hold onto these physical reminders of our past because remembering the dead is often easier than celebrating the living.

I lie under the unfulfilling weight of the comforter recalling the fleeting moments Violet and I used to lie in this bed together. She's cropped me out of her life, relegating me to an unseen corner of her room among the other various bits of clutter, like the junk cleaned out of drafts but never deleted, to be pulled up and placed in the story line where convenient. But she's not gone from mine. She pervades the heavy air, the tepid space where elbows used to touch in this now-empty bed. She's left me to carry her grief in the midst of my own mourning, to uphold the crumbling façade of it all. She's left me in the middle of her.

I sit up with her shadows, the shapes of her that flitter in and out, the sound of her that taps and creaks, whispers and screams. I sit up with the static in the air that gathers at my elbows and watch as it passes through the narrow doorway of this old house. I sit up with the dead in the room. I see their faces, hear their voices that stucco with choked diaphragms, dry mouths, spongy salted tears. But I do not join them.

THEY SHRINK FROM HARD WORK

n June 2, 1961, Beatrice Grover looked out the kitchen window to see smoke rising from one of the horse barns on the family's sixty-five-acre farm. She ran out of the house and up a short rise of grass to the barn and squeezed in through the sliding door. Flames whipped and cracked around her. She unlatched the gates of the three stalls and flung them open to let the horses out. The horses galloped into the field, unscathed. Beatrice ran back into the house and called the fire department. She grabbed her youngest son, David, and rushed back outside to make sure no other animals or children came near the blaze. The fire incinerated the barn and all the equipment inside, including her daughter Sharon's new show saddle.

Sharon was eleven years old and had just begun participating in her local 4-H saddle club, the Lucky Horseshoes. Beatrice was heartbroken, knowing she would have to tell Sharon that she wouldn't be able to compete in the upcoming season. Each of Beatrice and her husband William's eleven children raised a colt and livestock for 4-H when they reached the age of ten. Because the family had no money for a new saddle, Sharon would be the only one to have to wait to begin 4-H.

News of the fire and Beatrice's quick action to save the horses—including Duke, Sharon's new sorrel—made the local newspapers. The members of the Lucky Horseshoes raised $71 and surprised Sharon with a new silver-studded show saddle. Sharon and Duke placed runner-up in the junior division. Later that year at the county fair, Sharon would ride Duke in the club's horse square dance.

In an interview after the competition, Sharon told the local paper, "My horse and I are wonderful pals. We go riding almost every day. I have been training him myself. I'm very thankful that Mother saved him from our burning barn, and for our wonderful leaders and club members who made it possible for me to continue in 4-H." The article included a photo of Sharon sitting on Duke, wearing a cowgirl hat and smiling.

The year of the barn fire, Donnie, the oldest of Beatrice's children, was living with his wife and children in the modest ranch house he had just built at the edge of his family's land. When Donnie was younger, he not only raised his colt and livestock for 4-H, he served on the county judging team and appeared on the local station's Sunday evening program *Junior Fair.*

Donnie's sister Dolores helped him prepare for his cattle shows at the county fair. A photo in the local newspaper in October 1954 shows a young Dolores standing over a wheelbarrow holding a shovel. The caption reads, "Straw Boss—Pretty Dolores Grover of Carroll High School gives a hand to brother Donnie in preparation for his stock entries at the Fair . . . and that ain't hay." As Donnie, Dolores, and many of their siblings grew older, they transitioned to serving as 4-H camp counselors at Tar Hollow State Park deep in Ohio's Appalachian region.

Donnie would go on to raise his three daughters in the home he built. He raised them with horses on the ten acres he bought from his parents. Together, children and horses ranged through the winding hills and fields of family land. Behind the house, a steep hill dove into a deep creek valley where they would take the horses to drink. As the children grew up, the size of the farm shrank. Donnie and his wife, Ruth, sold land around the house to other families. The simple pole barn with the tin roof Donnie had built remained, but eventually the crops and livestock disappeared. So too did the horses.

Donnie's three daughters had nine children, and I grew up in the house he built with my parents, my two siblings, and my oldest first cousin. We roamed the land, up along the creek bed through forest and hill, or behind the neighbors' houses to the hill with the single tree where we'd watch the sun go down. I climbed the silver maple with the rope swing in the backyard, bringing supplies to create my own treetop world. We sledded down the hillside in winter, and if we had enough weight on the toboggan, we could often coast all the way to the creek, jumping out just before we splashed into the frozen water. My cousins and I played in the treehouse my grandfather built on the hillside, complete with functioning windows and my oldest cousin's artwork hanging inside. We lit bonfires year-round, lay under the stars, watched the combines plow, observed the long straight flight of the biplanes as they sprayed pesticide on the surrounding fields. Just beyond the cornfields sat my great-grandmother's house, more cousins, more family. Living with them was a link to the world before my birth.

My family was close, and I grew up much as they had done in and around a village of just a few hundred people, a settlement once famous for sitting at the intersection of the Hocking and Erie Canals. The village, boasting one traffic light, claims to be Lon Chaney's birthplace, though this is widely disputed. His parents might have stopped there on their way to Colorado and unexpectedly birthed him. Regardless of whether this was factual, it was true enough for the village.

Our village was Carroll: where we kids lined up on Wednesday afternoons in summer waiting for the firefighters to release the water on the fire hydrant so we could play in it; the town of the Old-Timers' Festival, featuring classic car shows, games, vendor tents, fair rides, and the yearly yard sale that was sometimes featured in the news. Across the highway that cut through the town stood a grain elevator, an old historic house, and a railroad bridge with "Class of '84" painted on it, the C and L faded through time. Our quaint village, with its two bars and one diner, a park in the shape of a triangle, a larger park, with a tall slide and a wooden merry-go-round, in a valley that floods, the gathering place for after-school hangouts and playground fights. The village where I'd walk with my cousin or friends to the convenience store next to the taxidermist to rent VHS tapes and buy candy bars, ice cream, and sandwiches.

I attended the same school my family had, going back generations. I attended classes in the same buildings and read from the same textbooks assigned by the same teachers. I came to see my older cousin play basketball in the same gym in which I'd later attend school plays, choir performances, and homecoming dances. I looked at my relatives' faces in the class photos that lined the hallway and filled the cafeteria and hoped to one day return and see mine beside them.

But when I picture the village, the countryside, and my family and their history, I don't see my face; I don't see my stories filling the landscape as theirs do. I can conjure the village and the landscape, describing it as bucolic and timeless. I can write general childhood memories about the village using the facts I've learned to try to make some claim to it. I can place a young me into that place in a way that's so generic I could be anyone. There's no substance to these memories, nothing compelling enough to leap off the page and rise to the level of a story. I don't have enough memories to draw on to fit the form, and I can't fake it without moving into the realm of fiction, without lying to myself, no matter how nice a story it would make, no matter how very rural or Appalachian these stories could present me.

I can't find or write myself there now, even when I have the chance to fill the narrative void. I left home and so my story in that village was cut short, and even though I planned to stay in that county forever, it didn't work out. I'd like to make this story of leaving home fit a tidy narrative. In this alternate narrative, I left to scrape by in major cities, but I miss home so I travel back as often as I can. I drive home to see my young cousins napping with their show animals, see the ribbons adorning their show squash, their pies, their quilts. I watch them ride horses and admire their prize heifers at competitions. In this fictional version of my life, we meet for dinner and pick up our relationships where we left off. I'd write a dramatic arc that would ease my guilt and hurt and unravel the threads of my emotional tension.

But I've never traveled home to see them. I have thought about looking for them, but I'm not sure what they do, what age they are now, as they are perpetually the last age at which I saw them, the last time we shared a life. I wouldn't know where to find them, or what we'd have in common. I don't even know if they're still home. And when I do finally drive home to see them in my real life, it's not at competitions or their houses, not for the holidays, not in any of the ways that could relieve this narrative of longing. Instead, I drive home for another funeral.

Sixty years after my great-grandmother saved the horses from the barn fire, after the photo of Sharon on her horse, after Donnie built the house in which he raised his children and grandchildren, I sit in front of his casket as relatives filter in and out of the room, sit and talk, reminisce, and admire the photos displayed around the room. My uncle David opens the service with a sermon and eulogy, and then the relatives eulogize my grandfather. Their stories touch on similar themes: my grandfather's unmatched work ethic, even at eighty-six; his love for my grandmother and his family. They speak of farming and animals and all the old ways Donnie embodied—all the things they too have come to embody because of him.

I sense the swirling of time, the circling of tradition, the restless entanglement of inheritance, land, memory, and tradition. All that binds and unbinds me sinks in the spaces between us. All I didn't learn, all that I could have become hides behind the tacky custard drapery and scutters across the ugly carpet. I try to absorb the details of the funeral, the stories and side conversations, the photos lining the walls. I try to muster inspiration from the depths of grief, to bring the meaning that death is supposed to endow on life and transform it into a story. Yet when my chance to speak comes, I fail to summon a memory of him that would mark me as the receiver of all he planted in us. Bearing witness would expose my shortcomings. Instead, I soak in my silence.

I want to insert into the narrative a tradition or artifact passed down to me to use as a metaphor to fill the void of experience, to wrap up the logic of the essay and impart a feeling. Again, I'm left wanting. I'd have to contrive or stretch a memory, which is why I often turn to the dead past, to the convenience of newspapers, where I can swiftly find accounts of German Appalachian traditions to suit my needs.

In the 1880s in Cincinnati, a boy was inexplicably dying. The women of the neighborhood diagnosed the boy as having been cursed by witches, as they had found a mysterious wreath made of straw and feathers in his bed. They salted and burned the wreath, and the boy recovered.

A few years later, another newspaper recounts, a man in Pittsburgh who had been ill for months threw his pillow away, claiming it was what made him sick. His wife, who had made the pillow, dismissed his claims, but after his death, she found a hard lump inside where a nest of feathers and straw had formed.

These mysterious nests found inside the pillows of people on their deathbed were called witch wreaths, death feather crowns, angel crowns, or death feather nests. They were often discovered by a family member noticing a hard lump in a pillow. Depending on the kind of nest, they portended different things. The circles of straw and feathers served as evidence of bewitchment and omens of death. Conversely, the crowns were symbols of salvation. Those who were fortunate enough to find them in their pillows were believed to have had their sins absolved. The wreaths meant that they were deserving of God's grace and would soon enter the pearly gates. It was believed that only the most deserving, those whose character and deeds in life were unparalleled in the community, those who held fast to faith and tradition, would merit these wreaths.

The tradition of pillow nests has disappeared almost entirely, possibly because the advance of scientific knowledge and rationalization brought an end to the belief in witches and curses, or because the industrialization of manufacturing pillows made of synthetic materials rendered handmade pillows unnecessary. Others claim that there are too few people left who keep the old ways, whose characters can hold the weight of tradition. The pillow nests that remain have ended up as family relics kept in boxes in closets and attics or inside glass domes on shelves, collecting dust.

In the funeral parlor, I consider the relatives who surround me, those who were raised right, maintained the old ways, and inherited the family line. All that our ancestors knew and passed down emanates from them. I've spent years reading and researching to learn all they know, hoping to meld with them. I turn to relics, photographs, and newspapers so that I can pull tradition out of the closet shoebox and hope that after years in the darkness it will imbue me with its powers. Writing has been an impulse to keep this past alive, to narratively construct myself as the inevitable inheritor of all that my ancestors created, all that I never learned. But I know my attempts are futile. I wouldn't need to work so hard to be convincing if I was there in the archive beside them. But I'm not there, and even if I stand on the highest peak in the county and scream my family name until the sandstone cliffs scream it back, my bones don't hold all my ancestors knew—and it's too late to inherit it now.

The family testifies to Donnie's character: his unmovable kindness, generosity, and joy, his unyielding faith. I imagine that a witch wreath appeared in his pillow, that while lying in bed in the live-in barn on his daughter's farm, he smiled, realizing he'd soon reap the reward for his good and long life. I hope to find a witch wreath in my pillow someday. But I never learned to make pillows of feathers and hay.

SALT RISING

PART ONE

The scream and moan of the dial-up echoed up the staircase to the kitchen where we were making hot tea and snacks, waiting to connect to the internet. While we prepared our dishes, we practiced our best feminine walks. Sonny sashayed the length of the kitchen in a few steps, and I scooted across the linoleum like Morticia Addams. We carried Sonny's grandmother's teacups down the stairs with straight backs and steady steps to keep the tea's surface undisturbed.

We had much to do online. We repeatedly checked our favorite website—the Evanescence band site—scrolling through the photos of Amy Lee, her handwritten lyrics, and the band. On Myspace, we updated our pages, found new codes for our backgrounds, embedded music, changed our photo slideshows, and rearranged our Top 8 friends. We chatted with our friends and complete strangers and kept up in the groups we had joined, dedicated to psychic vampires, Wicca, Anne Rice, and general goth content. We ran a small Evanescence group for Ohio fans where people posted about show locations, arranged carpools, and gave the scoop on where to find posters and T-shirts at stores like Hot Topic and Spencer's.

Talking to strangers on Yahoo! Chat Room was our favorite pastime. We made a dozen or so random profiles, but the ones we used for the longest were avatars we named PartyMonster and ChristinaSuperstar after one of our favorite films, *Party Monster*. Sonny idolized the fictional James St. James—gay, fabulous, witty, glamorous, always laughing and making the most of any situation that came his way. I was obsessed with Christina Superstar. Christina sang terribly and her constant drug use made her seem whimsical and random—in my favorite scene of her in the film, she drove a box truck around a parking lot to host a short-lived party in the trailer.

We pieced together our online personas from parts of ourselves, the characters we named ourselves after, and our visions for who we hoped to become. Sonny transformed into an older gay drag queen, while I was a woman with long black hair who dressed in the most high-feminine gothic clothing and exuded carelessness and charm. Our avatars protected us and gave us room to explore all we couldn't in our physical worlds.

But our avatars couldn't protect us in some digital spaces. In chat rooms labeled gay, lesbian, or transsexual, we got lost among cultural references we didn't understand and a vernacular we didn't share. We didn't have a language for our feelings, and when we tried to connect with others we were often shunned or kicked out of the groups for not knowing. Some groups labeled us pretenders, or just curious or questioning, in ways that shut down our curiosity and our questioning. Besides, the labels never quite fit.

Instead, we explored our nascent sexualities and gender identities on our own. We used our new personas to flirt with men we thought were boys. Often they'd send us photos and videos, and sometimes they'd show up nude on a webcam. Sometimes, if we couldn't get away from them quick enough, or if we turned down their advances, they would say terrible things to us, and because they were more knowledgeable about computers and the internet than we were, they would find us other places online and continue their harassment.

We expected our personas would receive attention offline if they were real, but we didn't want the negative kind we saw boys and men give to girls. Sonny wanted boys to find him as attractive as he found them, boys he couldn't find in our tiny school of a few hundred students. I found boys and girls attractive, and even though it didn't feel good, I wanted the attention girls received because somewhere in me, I knew it meant I was one, if only for a moment. This game we played felt innocent and fun, though later I would come to know how very troublesome it was. But when I tried to be ChristinaSuperstar offline, the harassment that couldn't reach past my screen could touch and harm me. In the uncertainty and confusion of cyberspace, at least I could exist in the correct body.

We protected our online world, our magic, giving it refuge by keeping the real world separate. Maybe someday, we imagined, we might release the pretending—my secret cross-dressing, Sonny's locked-room sashaying, our teatime housewifery—little by little into our offline world. But for years to come, we let the basement computer room, our cinder and glass block sanctuary, keep it all. In that room, the strange invisible world screamed to life on the screen, floated in the ether for a while, then disappeared. The digital world carried our burdens for us, and we could rest knowing that the next time we dialed up, our other selves would be waiting.

Cards lay in neat rows and stacks on the table, hands removed cigarettes in mouth to deposit ash into empty Coke cans, Mountain Dew bottles, or the ashtrays on the corners of the table. The card table wobbled and creaked, threatening to buckle under the weight of so many elbows. A game of Magic: The Gathering had been raging for hours. Creed played on the stereo from the corner of the room where others sat playing Xbox on the flatscreen. I watched from the kitchen through the built-in shelves at the edge of the counter where half-empty pizza boxes and red plastic cups sat stacked together. I poured Gatorade and plastic-bottle-vodka into red cups and walked across the yellow linoleum to the shaggy brown carpet, past the thick leather couches pushed up against wood paneling to deliver the drinks around the room.

We were in our early twenties, but Sonny was the only one of us who had his own place, a trailer in the community that bordered the new Walmart, which had bought out the old farmland next to the mall. We gathered there to play video games as well as the board games Magic: The Gathering and D&D, listen to music; and practice Pagan magic as a full coven. Sonny and I had been best friends since we met at school during gym on the track in fourth grade more than a decade earlier. Neither of us wanted to run the track, so we walked and talked instead. I had transferred to the village's public school from Christian school in fourth grade, and he was the first kid to treat me kindly and to get to know me. Our bond grew quickly, from spending lunch and all our time in the hallways together to riding the bus home to his house or mine after school most days. We normally made cheese sandwiches or some other easy-to-throw-together concoction before we locked ourselves into a room to play video games or ran off into the woods behind the barn to role-play.

One day at my house, after we made our sandwiches Sonny sat on the corner of the counter in front of the microwave. I leaned up against the counter by the sink. We ate in silence while I waited to see what he wanted to do, why we weren't moving to another room. Then he spoke quietly: *I think like boys.*

I know, I replied, laughing.

We ran to my room to play *Legend of Dragoon* on PlayStation, turned on the boombox to Evanescence's *Fallen*—which we'd been playing on repeat since it came out, since we went to the mall to see *Daredevil* just to hear the band in a theater—and never spoke of it again.

Sonny and I met most of our trailer park game group at the mall. Over the years we became fixtures of the Friday night food court, the parking lot outside the movie theater, the various alternative stores in the mall, the coffee shop owned by the goth woman who looked out for us. These were the friends who surrounded me the night I wore a dress for the first time around the mall, the night the Hot Topic manager told me to grow up and stop seeking attention. The group comforted me in the parking lot after I ran outside and paced the small patch of grass in the tree line across from the river. In the warm evening air, dusty from the crumbling parking lot, I finally said it out loud to the tree, to the river, to Sonny: *I think I'm a girl.*

I know, he replied, laughing.

The realization never came as a surprise to Sonny or the group because the goth subculture let us play and express our gender and sexual fluidity in its androgynous aesthetic.

Around the trailer each week, in the mall, in town, we wore Tripp pants, band Ts, long black dresses, chain wallets, pentagram belt buckles, ball chain necklaces, fishnets, sweat bands, platform boots, black sneakers, biker boots. We adorned ourselves with thick eyeliner, spiked gel hair, high pigtails, black, pink, blue, green, purple hair extensions, and of course the ubiquitous black nail polish.

In the shadow of Ohio's Allegheny plateau, we drew attention in a town where discount department store fashion and Midwest country were the norm. But we also didn't fit in with the other people we knew were different, the ones we called "rainbow emos" for the way they dressed—similarly to emo kids with tight clothes, coiffed hair, and bright color accents, but with rainbow belts, sweat bands, pins, suspenders, shoelaces. They drove to the big city to attend gay events and go to bars and clubs. They loved dance and club music. The culture that they connected through—the art, music, literature—centered on being LGBT. They made references to New York City and San Francisco, places called Stonewall and the Castro.

We didn't understand their cultural references or the histories they cited, histories that didn't seem to include us. We knew about Matthew Shepard, victim of a rural small-town experience we all dreaded would happen to us, but not much else. They too spoke with a different vocabulary. They constantly criticized and drew attention to each other, but in ways that made them laugh. According to them we didn't speak the right language or wear the right clothing. And

our references, our shared understanding of our gender and sexuality—genderless vampires, humans that morphed their genders or
into other creatures—were devoid of meaning to them. They were
metaphorical at best, and at worst they were insulting to *actual*
LGBTQIA people, which did not include us, not *actually*. They
labeled us hicks, though we thought the same of them, masking
their trash under rainbows as we did under black fishnets.

When we traveled to the big city for concerts and to visit goth
clubs, we didn't fit in even with our fashion because we looked like
white trash, or we tried too hard, only doing what was popular,
wearing what we could buy at the mall but not what was *really*
alternative. To goths in the big city, we were poor imitations. We
weren't hicks, at least we didn't think we were, but again, the goth
history that traced back to a small club in England, to New York
City, and to Los Angeles, didn't include us. No matter where we
turned, the world seemed to push us away.

So Sonny's house became our sanctuary.

At the stereo I picked a new CD to put on from the stack of albums:
Evanescence, My Chemical Romance, Creed, Otep, Rob Zombie. I
put on *Three Cheers for Sweet Revenge* and the room broke out in
an off-key but full-chested rendition of "I'm Not Okay (I Promise)."
I sat on the couch and watched the video game on the flatscreen
as black pants touched black pants, painted nails moved between
game controllers and drinks, fishnet sleeves wrapped around necks
covered with chainmail necklaces, and I knew we weren't missing
out on life outside the trailer park, beyond the old crumbling town,
the crumbling hills. We had forged a space that didn't require explanation, where we didn't have to prove anything, where our history
and references and language were ours, created together.

I met Levi at the mall as he came out of the coffee shop owned by
the goth woman who looked out for the mall rats. My friend and I

were wearing bright barrette clips in our hair, and as Levi passed us, he pulled his hand out of his bag to show more clips. *I like your barrettes. Here, you can have these!*

We took the clips and put them in our hair next to the others. I grabbed a napkin from a holder, wrote on it "Barrette Bitches Anonymous," and handed it to him. *We made a Myspace group about hair clips. You should join.*

Our Myspace group only had two members before Levi joined. The idea started after my friend gave me a clip to hold my hair back, and we decided to wear matching clips every day at school. I added Levi to my Top 8 on Myspace soon after we met. I was too shy to talk to him on Myspace, but I hoped to see him again.

A while later, I went with my brother to the music store in town. He wanted to go to look for CDs, and I'd heard they had posters and buttons and patches of bands I followed. We browsed for a while and then I noticed the cashier: bright colors and long blond hair.

Oh, hi. Do you work here?

Just in the evenings sometimes. My dad owns the place.

I smiled and pointed to the barrettes he'd given me, and before I left, he handed me a candy bracelet. I wore it daily for a week, protecting it against classmates trying to get a candy off or snap the elastic band before I finally left it at home on my dresser altar, next to the incense holder, the pentagram, the offerings of flowers, the ritual wand and knife. Later I wrapped it around a candle that I burned for him.

Months later, at a cafeteria-style restaurant/Japanese techno nightclub, I saw Levi and his father standing in line. I waited until he turned around and then, with my hand pressed tight against my chest, I waved with my fingers. He came to me, holding his tray. *My dad comes here to source stuff for his store, and I love to eat here. Get this bento box, you'll like it and it's all vegan. Aren't you?*

I'm vegetarian. I've only been here once so you'll have to help me order.

He accompanied me to the counter and explained all the different ingredients in detail—where they were from, how they were prepared, their proper pronunciations. Levi was a gateway to all things Japanese. He wrote to pen pals in Japan and studied the language and culture, visiting in summers when he could. We ate together and talked about Japan and electronic music, the friends we had in common, the parks we liked to visit. We made plans to meet.

A week later, Levi met me at my house. He was wearing orange parachute pants and a long-sleeved shirt under a bright tie-dyed short-sleeved one. He had on round glasses and bright plastic and candy bracelets. He'd painted his nails bright primary colors and he wore barrette clips that matched mine, the ones he'd given me. His blond hair touched the concrete behind him as he sat on the steps outside my house.

We drove to our favorite arboretum which, among the wetlands, teaching areas, and settler cemeteries, had a Japanese-style garden. We walked around the Japanese garden, and I listened to Levi tell me about the design, where the trees came from, why the garden was installed, its importance, the reasons he loved it. We held hands as we walked and I watched him smile, transfixed by the light reflecting off the gold rim of his glasses. The air around us sank heavy in the summer heat, filling the space between us. The sap of the pines and the pollen grew around us in one buzz, swelling and morphing, making me dizzy.

We walked across the Japanese bridge over the pond to a little gazebo to sit in the shade and eat the food he'd prepared for our picnic: rice, tofu, bok choy, sushi. He demonstrated the proper way to hold chopsticks and I watched how easily he maneuvered the food. I noticed the way he didn't show his teeth when ate, the way he held his hand over his mouth and laughed when he noticed me staring at him. He pulled out a jug of red Kool Aid from his bag and we drank it all down, hot after the day in the sun. I wanted to tell him there was still red on the sides of his lips, but I also wanted it there, hoping I might taste it later.

We left the Japanese garden, moving to a shaded patch of grass under a dense grove to lie and stare at the sky, the clouds, the underside of the treetops. Levi rolled from side to side, laughing, and I heard the swish of the Kool Aid in his stomach and joined in. This rolling and laughing led to hand holding and, after the clouds above us had cleared the tree line, a small, quiet, impossibly soft, red kiss.

As we walked back to the car, holding hands, the sun set lower behind the trees and the air felt stickier, more alive with the early buzz of crickets and cicadas. The trees danced and swayed: sweating, breathing. We stood on the wooden dock over the amphibian preserve out of sight of the parking lot and the few visitors there. In that fragrant shade, I hoped for another kiss, but he dropped my hand and walked to the edge of the dock. He stared down at the bubbling, dark green, viscous liquid full of salamander egg sacs. His hair fell over his face and caught the rays of light filtering through the canopy. His polished fingernails tugged at his striped sleeves as he fidgeted, and he tapped the end of one bright Converse on the wood. He spoke softly, almost inaudibly. *I'm not sure how this will work out. I like spending time with you, but I'm not gay.*

Well, I'm not a boy, I replied, laughing.

Levi shrugged, considering my words, then took my hand in his again as we walked to my mother's minivan, which I had borrowed for the day. We rolled the windows down, adorned ourselves with sunglasses and neck pillows my mother kept in the van, opened Ramune drinks, and set out. We listened to a mix CD I'd made for him—Portishead, Birthday Massacre, Hungry Lucy. As we drove, I glanced at his long hair blowing out the window and stared as the sun, that hot orange glow, overtook the rearview mirror. The trees tugged and tumbled in waves from the teetering hillsides behind us as we drove—hill after hill, field after field—home, together.

The cover of the magazine read, *What Is Goth?* centered in white script on a solid black background. The issue opened with the history of the goth subculture, then transitioned into interviews with students in my high school. Photos of the group were intermingled with the text. In the main photo, I stood wearing black Tripp pants with green trim, A Perfect Circle's *Thirteenth Step* T-shirt over a long-sleeved black fishnet shirt, a black choker with crisscrossed chains, lots of rings, and black gel band bracelets. My girlfriend stood beside me next to our best friend and two of our other friends. We were the "kids in black"—the vampires, the weirdos, the killers and, incorrectly, the emos—the goth kids of our tiny rural school.

The five of us stood out so prominently that the school paper dedicated a special issue to exploring the "goth presence" at our high school. We gave them a reason to. We were always together at school, in the hallways before class and at lunch in the courtyard or arboretum. We gathered in the park outside the school, at the mall, and in our houses. The rumors around the school and village were that we practiced sex magic, Satanic blood rituals, dark Wiccan magic. People thought we'd shoot up the school because our floor-length trench coats from Hot Topic, obviously inspired by *The Matrix,* made people inaccurately reference the Columbine massacre. We were very depressed, after all. One of us was even rumored to have posted a list of classmates we wanted to sacrifice on Myspace—a rumor that, while true, referred to the straight-A, wealthier student who headed the school's Teen Institute and other clubs.

We didn't mind the attention or the protection that came with being read as mysterious. We figured the misunderstanding came from not really associating with other students who weren't in our group, and from not meeting publicly in the same places our classmates frequented. And perhaps because of the supposed combination dark spell book/kill list we shared. We passed this notebook in the hallway at school or left it in each other's lockers in between classes. Teachers frequently confiscated it and looked it over, but ultimately returned it to us. This spell book was a menacing, pink, five-subject, college-ruled notebook decorated in handwritten script reminiscent of Fraktur. Teary eyes, skulls, and pentagrams surrounded the writing.

Inside the notebook, we wrote song lyrics, parts of poems, random meanderings, thoughts on new albums and art. We drew art and doodles inside or attached printouts of art from sites like VampireFreaks and DeviantArt. We wrote quotes from our favorite films. Our favorite, and the one that frequently sent us to the school counselor, came from the film *Ginger Snaps*: "Out by sixteen or dead on the scene, but together forever." Which only gave most of us about a year to live. We also left messages for the teachers who would read our notebook looking for signs that we were going to cause trouble, evidence of our depression and self-harm.

Another reason we figured we garnered such attention came from the fact that we were openly not heterosexual or cisgender. Our understanding of ourselves and our relations remained undefined. The words we found to use were just shorthand that didn't capture the feeling of our lives together, but we deployed and returned them as needed. We learned the words *pansexual* and *asexual,* and I came across the word *transsexual* in a medical encyclopedia in the school library, but I didn't think I fit the category. I used *androgynous* and *cross-dresser.* But we tended to just say that we were not straight.

We had many classmates who were out and proud, and we did interact with them sometimes, although we didn't become friends with them. We joined them to fight against the Christian group led by teachers who lectured us all about our sexual sins, about our need to come to Christ. We campaigned against them and the administration to allow same-gender partners to attend prom and other school events together. There were more socially open teachers, but to them our sexuality still came off as deviant, for shock value, not something we truly were, a hindrance to the gay students' fight for equality, for normality.

Behind these rumors and stories told about us, our activities weren't all that mysterious or different from our classmates'. We weren't newsworthy. We lounged in basements listening to music, watching TV, reading. We lay out in the grass and open fields staring at the stars. We threw things at the side of barns, at dead trees, at the junk cars and scrap metal that filled so many yards. We drank in barns, smoked in barns, had sex in barns. We wandered the dark woods that led nowhere. We dreamed of escape, of never leaving. And in the dark of night, around bonfires under bright moons, we made pacts to stay together forever.

PART TWO

I've held these memories as snapshots of my lost community, moments I've long wanted to relive. Nostalgia constitutes part of this longing, as does the cleaving I've experienced in my sense of self. I've lived in cities for half my life, and I miss the countryside, the very fabric of my worldview. I'm desperate for the freedom and creativity of a time before the rampant drive of metropolitanism seeped into everything, before I became inundated with—implicated in—discourse.

I can't return to that time, yet given my wish to preserve all that the country made me, there's little room for me in the metropolis with its heightened visibility and homogenous vision of transgender life. The promise of a metropolitan community remains unfulfilled. I've only found people with emptiness reaching for the emptiness in others, hoping to fill it with a label, a code, a shared something. So I scoured my memories for meanings, for clues about how to recapture that community, one that might have been queer and transgender and Appalachian, my utopia, my refuge. All I found were fantasies.

It's easy to imagine that community exists in Appalachia, because the concept of community in the United States is often embodied in idyllic small towns, like the village of nearly four hundred people that my friends and I grew up on the outskirts of. These small towns are often imagined as places where a small group of people interact closely with one another and share similar values, interests, and identities. Everyone has their place within the order of small-town life and all unite to care for one another. In these small towns people pursue a different, slower way of living that hails from a time long before the present, some era when people noticed and cared for one another. Thus rural small towns in the US are imagined not only as places but also as times.

The place of Appalachia likely exists deep in the natural landscape, where one's ancestors might have grown up, or the place where family land has been passed down, or taken, or lost to corporate environmental degradation. This Appalachia is likely rural, mountainous, most definitely not a populous city. This Appalachia exists inside a hollow, a holler, a hillside, the valley of a mountain range, and likely contains sulfur creeks and crumbling barns, trailer parks, and rundown houses with junk in the front yard.

Similarly, the time of this imagined Appalachia exists in childhood or the time of ancestors, of grandparents, most certainly a time before the technology of today, the time when folkways were still practiced, the time of sitting on front porches and grandmothers cooking Sunday suppers, the time of town events, of culture. A time when rugged people fought against extraction and the government, the metropolis, dominant society, the future, to preserve their way of living.

The idea of my lost Appalachian community flourished on my family land outside a small town and a trailer park in the valley of mountains before technology was integrated into every facet of my existence. My Appalachian community existed in adolescence, before I even knew that Appalachia—the problems facing it and the national discourse surrounding it—existed.

But basing the concept of community on shared ways of living and identities offers only a flimsy foundation. The Appalachia of the national imagination—the one I am attempting to reconstruct through setting my memories to page—builds on stereotypes and assumptions about the region's history.

In *The First American Frontier: Transition to Capitalism in Southern Appalachia, 1700–1860,* Appalachian historian Wilma Dunaway writes that these stereotypes and assumptions come from what she calls the nation's "long running love affair and romance" with the region tracing back to eighteenth-century Jeffersonian ideals about rugged individualism. These ideals, based on the myth that frontier America was egalitarian and offered upward mobility, were epitomized by the "Jeffersonian folk hero," the "yeoman farmer" who was honest and fiercely self-sufficient, forging through action the foundation of the promise of democracy. In the nineteenth and twentieth centuries, these ideals persisted as commentators portrayed Appalachia as frozen in time, a homogenous world of folk societies still adhering to the old frontier ways.

These narratives did not exist solely as rhetoric; they caused deep and long-lasting material effects in the region. Researchers of varying backgrounds came to the region in the 1920s to study the physiological, social, and geographic makeup of Appalachia as part of a nationwide project to track genetic traits by region. The goal was to propose eugenic measures to counter bad breeding, which eugenicists thought led to delinquency, criminality, and psychopathy. Researchers used their findings to teach social workers and medical students the latest in eugenics theory during the 1920s and '30s. These studies had negative effects on the region. Physicians lobbied legislators for laws allowing the involuntary sterilization of sex offenders, habitual criminals, epileptics, the "feebleminded," and "hereditary defectives."

The findings of this brand of research were enacted into law in places like Virginia in 1924, the same year as the Racial Integrity Act, which reinforced racial segregation by prohibiting interracial marriage. Other legislation passed at the time culminated in the forced sterilization of nearly eight thousand people in Virginia alone, mostly Black women. The use of this law by the State of Virginia was tested in *Buck v. Bell*, heard before the Supreme Court in 1927. Oliver Wendell Holmes delivered the Court's opinion upholding the legality of eugenic sterilization, which included the infamous phrase "three generations of imbeciles are enough."

As the twentieth century progressed, the notion that poverty and vagrancy were associated with defective heredity shifted as researchers began to recognize that the reasons for failure to succeed in society had to do with something beyond genetics. Where eugenicists saw the inheritance of bad genes, sociologists began to see a vicious cycle of poverty and lack of opportunity. This shift away from material eugenics, however, did not translate to research that looked to dismantle the social structures causing poverty in Appalachia. Instead, in 1965, the Johnson administration's "War on Poverty" created the Appalachian Regional Commission (ARC). The commission, defining this geographic region as a coherent political entity, sought to monitor and create economic development in Appalachia. The ARC assigned each county in Appalachia a score based on a scale of economic distress in order to administer federal aid where it was most needed. The ARC rhetorically and materially mapped Appalachia, just as the eugenics researchers had before them, as a region defined by poverty, and subsequently poverty came to be defined by the region, which was described in government research and academic publications according to anthropologist Oscar Lewis's "culture of poverty" theory: penury had so shaped the individual psyches and value systems of people living in poverty that the condition was endlessly perpetuated.

These narratives haven't changed much in the twenty-first century. Contemporary narratives portray the Appalachian region as both the quintessential America, what is best about the nation, and as a place of deviance and backwardness. At the same time, major newspapers publish op-eds that depict Appalachia as the symbol of everything wrong with the country. In his piece for the *New York Magazine* titled "No More Sympathy for the Hillbilly," Frank Rich writes that the presence of "Trumpists" in Appalachia justifies cutting the region off from the rest of the country. "Let them reap the consequences for voting against their own interests," Rich suggests. Writers like Rich establish contemporary Appalachia as the region of the archetypal hillbilly, a character of backward politics, then concluding that the solution to our region's issues is to just allow us to be isolated, suffering, and poor.

That poverty defines Appalachia as a region is one of what Emily Satterwhite, professor of Appalachian studies, calls the "five myths of Appalachian exceptionalism." The other four are "Appalachia is all rural and the most rural part of the country; Appalachia is all white and the whitest place in the United States; Appalachia is all mountains; Appalachia is pre-modern." The long-standing stereotypes of Appalachia generally touch on all five of these myths.

I add a six myth of Appalachian exceptionalism to Satterwhite's list: Appalachia is all cisgender and heterosexual and the most cisgender, heterosexual place in the United States. This myth also follows the contradiction inherent in the public imaginary of Appalachia: the region with the most heteronormative people in the country and the place of the most deviant, backward, and violently queer sexual and gender proclivities.

These stereotypes are so deeply embedded into the ways we conceive of the region that in taking shared identity, values, or interests and activities as bases for community means that rural places, especially Appalachia, are excluded from being the sites of queer and transgender life. Instead, urban locations become the sole loci for queer and transgender communities, and queer and transgender people's flight from rural locations to cities seems inevitable, even compulsory. This is in part because the historical circumstances of queer liberation in cities made identity a necessary category, and these identities had to be visible in some way.

This visibility and proximity allowed the spaces in cities generally associated with queer people to form—districts, bars, nightclubs, coffee shops, community centers. The people who gathered in these places shared an identifiable subculture. Then notable events like Stonewall and ACT UP brought visibility to the queer liberation movement, and over time the notion of queer people as "out, loud, and proud" became an acceptable queer typology.

The anthropologist Kath Weston confirms this history. In her article in *GLQ*, "Get Thee to a Big City: Sexual Imaginary and the Great Gay Migration," Weston writes that the stereotype of the rural/urban divide "locates gay subjects in the city while putting their presence in the countryside under erasure." She documents that when rural queers arrive in cities and find these supposed queer havens, they are often disappointed and alienated. This is because "the gay imaginary is not just a dream of a freedom to be gay that requires an urban location, but a symbolic space that configures gayness itself by elaborating an opposition between urban and rural life." To flourish in the metropolis, the community there needs a backward place like Appalachia to exist to define itself against. The deeply felt effect of this binary is that queer and transgender people who live in rural areas, or who have moved to major cities but retain a deep love and attachment to their home regions and people, are told that they are not fully queer or transgender, and that they invite whatever alienation or violence they experience.

Even stories that purport to show the vibrance of life in the region or highlight the lives of people who have moved out of Appalachia take part in these stereotypes about rural queer people. Some focus on the tragedies of rural life, thus reifying and relocating queer violence into rural spaces. Other narratives focus on why people "choose to stay" in Appalachia and thus reinscribe Appalachia as a place queer people are supposed to flee. Often these narratives appear when queer people talk about moving back home or "queering" their home region by bringing a metro queer lifestyle back to the rural area. Though these queer narratives aim to portray the region positively—referencing the agrarian myth, citing histories of resistance, egalitarianism, closeness to the land, and older, better ways of living—they still frame queer life falsely, as metropolitan versus rural, overlook a long history of visible queer and transgender life in rural places, and obscure the fact that for many queer and transgender people, moving from cities to rural places offered an escape from what was often actually the inability to live how they wanted in urban spaces.

The historian Emily Skidmore writes about this history in her book *True Sex: The Lives of Trans Men at the Turn of the Twentieth Century.* Skidmore examines newspaper archives to follow transgender men at the turn of the twentieth century as they moved from urban to rural locations, often with partners, to live normal, unassuming lives. They were not hiding or struggling to exist. They were known by their neighbors and they and their partners were often profiled by local and national press. Skidmore shows how local newspapers and their small-town readership were tuned into national discourses but also forged their own understandings of gender and sexuality, historical realities that don't align with how we in the present presume the people of the past lived. Skidmore writes that contrary to our modern understanding of trans people in rural areas, not all lived as part of "a tight-knit community that shared an underground lifestyle," but "existed out in the open." They were "not always urban rebels who sought to overturn normative gender roles" but often sought perfectly unexceptional lives in out-of-the-way places. The trans men and their partners that lived in these areas usually did not find trouble with their neighbors or any hindrances to their lives unless they stopped participating in rural ways of living, which could come in the form of a perceived inability to provide for the household, a reliance on charity when inappropriate, inciting religious provocations, or dropping out of shared hard work and communal living.

The experiences of the trans individuals in rural areas that Skidmore explores mirror those that I had growing up in small-town Ohio. I never felt that our sexualities or genders were as disruptive as our participation in an alternative subculture and our refusal to participate in—indeed, our outright antagonism toward—important social activities. We refused to stand for the pledge of allegiance or the national anthem. We openly bashed our school's football team. We mocked George W. Bush, the Christian church, the FFA kids, the military guests who visited school. We attended events where we visibly didn't fit in just to disrupt them. We didn't want to work on the land or do manual labor. We stayed inside too much, playing music and making art. Worst of all, we kept to ourselves, and our interests and our values didn't fit normative rural standards.

I selected these memories to show that I didn't have unprecedented or unique experiences in Appalachia devoid of influences from other places, and that is not unusual. These memories also serve narrative functions, allowing me to connect myself back to an Appalachian history I didn't know I had at the time. The worlds I've re-created don't align with the myths of Appalachian exceptionalism central to the national imagination of the region, and nor do they mirror metropolitan visions of queer and transgender life, so they serve to alter the standard perceptions of life in Appalachia. On a personal level, these memories let me relive what felt like community. We fashioned a way of life from what was available to us in our region, county, and group of friends.

Maybe that's behind my impulse to recover and transplant my memories into my contemporary life. I look to them as blueprints for rural metropolitan living. I look to them for healing. But why would I long to capture a community built around queer, transgender, or Appalachian identities after laying bare the myths that construct them?

I must long for community because it feels older than society and modernity, older than capitalism, or at least my awareness of it. I want to return to the community of my past because the past was better, and the present era gets worse as time goes by because the unceasing and rapid change, the alienating bureaucracy and rampant consumerism of capitalism have destroyed any sense of connection. Maybe I see community as a solution to capitalism. But I know that this too is a myth.

Capitalism breaks down basic human relations—our desires, rules, ethics, codes of behavior—putting our worlds into chaos. It strips us from ourselves and others. Once we feel isolated and wanting, we are in better positions to have things sold to us to fill the void. We get offered an array of increasingly specific and rigid identities. We are sold interests, activities, fashions, ways of living that align with these new identities. We become so unlike everyone around us.

When it comes to identities like Appalachian, we must look a certain way, speak within an acceptable range of dialects and accents. We must hail from a particular family line of mythic mee-maws, granny witches, strong mountain mamas, and resolute coal-mining men who were also probably 'shiners. We should hunt, fish, and farm. We must listen to bluegrass and take part in quaint folkways. We certainly care about coal.

In trans and queer circles, there's a certain vernacular, an attention to fashion, or living a DIY lifestyle. One must like drag, ball culture, the club scene, follow the lives of rich white women, be deeply involved in philosophy and politics, engage with specific films, books, music, and underground zines. There are histories and lineages we must learn and cite.

We cling to all that we've been sold after everything else has been stripped away, hoping to become secure and logical within the chaos, to gain a sense of self. These identity categories become irreconcilable differences, gaps too deep and fundamental to bridge. When we finally reach out of our isolation to find others, they tend to hold these same understandings of themselves and the same beliefs, interests, and activities, and the difference between what we expect to find in them and what we find only causes more dissonance.

We often can't perform or uphold the identity category, and if we step outside the boundaries of the group, or if we question the categories of group identification and their enforcement, we can be met with hostility. Internally, we come to feel that something is fundamentally wrong with us. We end up wanting what we want to want, no longer knowing what we want or need. We just do what fits the scene. We follow the rules and more division occurs, which capitalism wants.

Thus community, as I've come to understand it, only complements capitalism. The groups I took part in were formed with a narrow range of ages, backgrounds, experiences, identities, beliefs, and activities. Inclusion within them was based on strict boundaries that were internally and externally enforced. I recognize that the communities I experienced in my home region were not communities at all, but scenes.

When I try to claim the scenes I've inhabited as communities, I foreclose on the possibility of growing and shifting as a person by locking myself into a rigid field of belonging. If I continue to only want the things that the scene wants, I risk losing some part of myself, my identity. Had I not left those scenes, as precious as they were to me, I wouldn't have formed new relationships with others and with myself that allow me to live more fully than I could have then.

If I claim the scenes I inhabited as communities, I also foreclose on that same possibility for others who inhabit them. I reduce my friends to only one facet of their existence, like their sexualities and genders or subcultures. I must leave out any complexity that challenges the uniformity of the whole. In doing this, I flatten all those I knew into caricatures of themselves and trap them in that time forever.

I mentally foreclosed on the possibility of real community before I even began writing this essay. The closest I've come to experiencing true community was the time I spent at church in the big city. Our church was filled with people of different ages from varying backgrounds, cities, neighborhoods, identities, experiences, and even beliefs. Yet when families needed housing, my siblings and I were stuffed into one room or the basement to make space for them. How easily my bedroom or the living room could turn into a hospice for grieving families. How many backyard memorials did we attend, marked by the memorial T-shirts that line dresser drawers in my childhood home? Even if we'd never see the people again, even if we had nothing else in common.

I struggle to reconcile the realization that I may have had a community in a place that had nothing to do with my gender, sexuality, or cultural identities. I did not include my church experiences because I did not maintain the religion after I left the church. My memories of church feel more distant, harder to recall. I attended church in the big city and not in my home region, and I have no real memories of being transgender or queer while at church. So these memories don't lend themselves to a trajectory that writes me into a queer, transgender, Appalachian past. They don't fit the grand narrative I'm constructing of myself. And I toss aside a whole group of people who helped to shape me when I leave out these memories. I don't give any of those people the possibility of being otherwise.

I've clung to the idea of my lost queer Appalachian community because I know deep down that I've never experienced one. I thought writing essays might guide me around this impasse. Writing has in part been about making sure the past doesn't die. I want to make the present more livable, to scramble timelines and carry the past into the endless future.

I searched my past for my lost community, and for a while I thought I had found it, the missing piece of the puzzle, the ballygilly to heal my feral heart. Those with whom I experienced these moments were friends, lovers, kin, chosen kin, and family, but they weren't my community. We didn't use that word to label what we had, and it wouldn't solve anything to commit the crime of presentism and do it now.

I can't reconstruct my memories or experiences. I can't continue striving toward regaining what I once had in them. And that's okay. If this witnessing, this testifying, has offered me something to use to fight off the ever-growing beast of urbanization, of capital eating at everyone and everything, and connect with others, it is the knowledge that there's nowhere I can look for community in my past. Everything I need to make one is here in front of me. That place which is also a time is this one.

A Roof, and Bed, and Board

My life began in a barn. Or at least I'd like to write that it did. I'd give a dramatic story of a birth in the hay surrounded by women. I would be kept warm by the livestock while the women took care of my mother or went back to work in the fields. The barn of my mythic birth could do work for me, turning my mundane childhood into a tale of becoming semi-feral, a rural wild child who would rather spend time alone with the animals in the barn or in the adjoining fields than with people. The barn could transform into a symbol of my rurality, my abandon, my uncouth nature, and to some extent that would be true. What would be truer to say is that most of my earliest memories involve barns, and that I spent much of my adolescence in them. But the barns of my youth do similar work for me.

Barns provided me space to meet and transform. Inside the horse barn beside a crumbling Victorian house, I stared up at the close angle of the roof and watched the ribbons of dust twirl and move, swarm, wave, and shift in the light. The air hung still as the heat of the day moved through the open space of the loft, over the hay, over the stacked bales, loose and scattered. The room rested quiet, the silence interspersed with the smack of horse tail and the irregular passing of cars, the small whirl of the cupola fan. In the loft lay candle lanterns, folding chairs, a cooler, a cassette radio, blankets, pillows. Posters and photos hung on the walls. Spent soda cans and food wrappers were strewn about with changes of clothes and other household items. My cousin and I stacked the hay bales to make walls, couches, beds, tables—a whole room just for us. We took the portable black-and-white television to the loft, trying to tune into something, anything. The barn became our hideaway, a secret mansion, a medieval war camp, a cave, a prayer nave, a refuge, a haunted attic. And it was also just a barn loft in a barn on the small flat above a rolling hill surrounded by corn, some grass, a rolling hill dotted with clover, a small cut of a creek, trees. It was a barn surrounded by other barns, other places to hide and be hidden.

A county over, I spent hours with my cousin in the barn his family lived in while rebuilding the farmhouse, where my grandfather moved after my grandmother died. In the upstairs bedroom there was a hole in the floor that looked down to the kitchen. I would lay flat on my stomach and peer through the hole, watching my aunt cook and hoping to be her someday.

The barns of my home county provided places to dwell with animals. Just through the creek valley and up the hill from my home stood my great-grandmother's barn where we often went to be near the horses. We snuck them food, sat on the ground and let them nudge our faces and nibble our hair. We wished to ride them free in the fields and off into the hazy sunset. We watched the other animals in the barn—the goats and barn cats—filter in and out. I lay on my back and watched the barn swallows as they nested in the corners and jumped and swooped around the barn, chirping.

I knew that birds served a practical function in barns, eating bugs and acting as alarm bells when danger was present. There is an architectural feature in barns named after barn swallows: *Schwalme-Loch*, or swallow holes, small apertures in the upper level of the barn that provide ventilation and allow the birds to move in and out. They are often decorative, cut in the shape of crosses, hearts, crescent moons, or diamonds. The presence of barn swallows in barns was also an auspicious sign to the Pennsylvania Dutch. They were thought to bring healthy crops and fattened livestock. The birds reminded me to be still, to give them space and to take up less myself. Even in the expanse of silence and stillness, they reminded me I was not alone.

Out my bedroom window, just beyond the flowerbeds, stood a small, tin-roofed pole barn my grandfather built. Inside was a dirt floor and tools for farming, fixing cars, and gardening. To escape the heat of the day I hid inside. I brought water to the many barn cats.

In the summer rain I sat with the door open and listened to the downpour on the tin roof. Out the door I watched as rainfall filled the creek valley, flowing down the streets and flooding the hills. The lilac branches bobbed and broke in the rain. I jumped as the lightning cracked above the sycamores. Inside that barn I felt timelessness, the creeping backward of all that came before, all that my ancestors built.

When we were teens, barns became spaces to get away from the stress of school and work, or the lack of work, or too many people living in one cramped house. Barns gave us spaces to pass away the boredom of having nothing to do with enough time and space to do anything. On Halloween, family and friends gathered on the farm for hayrides, a bonfire, food and drink. We grabbed booze from the ice buckets and snuck past the old metal signs and antique tools on the barn wall to the space between the barn and the greenhouse. In the cool night air, we lamented the nothingness of our lives, the void that draped around us. In the encroaching expanse of cornfield, silence, and trees, the barns we met in provided us space away from the adults to grieve or celebrate the present and plan our futures together.

As I grew older, barns became places for me to dream, plan, reminisce. I visited my grandfather on the farm and sat in a recliner, listening to him tell stories about his parents, his grandparents, the farm, his life before mine. The barns of my adolescence became places to recharge and remind myself that I had a place to come back to, a place to work toward, or at the very least a place to fantasize about returning to, knowing I'd be unlikely ever to return. Because after I left home for the big city, most of the barns I had known were torn down, too unstable to maintain, too unnecessary. Some were replaced with houses or fields, and some were left to decay into the earth. The crops disappeared and the farms dissolved. The barns that remained were emptied of most of their animals, even the birds, as there was nothing left for them to bless.

No matter how long I've lived in a major city, and no matter the memories I have and continue to form, I long to recapture the memories and emotions of the times I spent in the barns of my home region. Adolescence was a time marked by heightened emotion and a slowing of time, so part of this longing must be nostalgia, a desire for a time and a self that are gone to time. But I've had emotional connection in the city, formed a decade of memories there, so I know my longing cannot be just about the emotion and connection, or even just the animals.

I'm also invested in the barns as structures. I have a deep interest in the movement to restore them or erect new ones built in the old way. I want to preserve the past for the future. But I know that barns, based on the memories of the emotions I've experienced within them, are not only structures but symbols. I can't shake loose the remnants of my adolescence, my view of the land and farms and the rural landscape. Everything I hold dear seems to be invested in barns. When they crumble into the ground or disappear entirely, a piece of me remains stuck inside them, gone forever, like my way of life, my childhood, my very self. I want to explore this feeling, to trace it back to where it became so deeply embedded in me. I start at the beginning.

In his book *Landscape in Sight,* the essayist and cultural geographer J. B. Jackson posits that land ownership is foundational to the concept of citizenship in the US. The land available for purchase was divided by the grid system, which was based on the "disregard of topography, the assumption that all pieces of land of the same size had the same value." He suggests that all one must do is look at a map or the landscape from above to see that land in the US unfolds in a series of large squares, regardless of the type of terrain. The townships of my home county are laid out in mostly uniform squares, as are the cities and towns within them.

The steps to get from rich and varied terrain to uniformity in the landscape seem straightforward to trace. Colonial settlers must turn the land and the people on it into resources to be harnessed. The first step is to eliminate Indigenous peoples from the land in a variety of ways, from outright genocide to removal and confinement in reservations outside of the ever-changing boundaries of white settlements. Assimilation and landowner acts are interlocking steps. Assimilation seeks to violently transform Native people into normative Western citizens by refiguring how people function in relation to land and how the land functions in the new physical and social order. Landowner acts establish a set of rules that govern who can own and sell this property, usually organized around an idea of citizenship. This process must fully erase and keep invisible any way of living that sees land and people as inextricable, co-nourishing, symbiotic.

Colonial settlers usually turn to the long-held views of land brought with them from feudal Europe. Thus farmsteads, with barns at the center of them, become central to this mission. Barns mark the land as space occupied for agriculture, store equipment and grain, and keep animals safe, all within view of the dwelling structure. The newly refigured land and its resources must be protected from change through physical measures, so fences, walls, and symbolic natural markers like lilac and rose bushes mark the land as inhabited by settlers.

After establishing the physical system by which to transform the land, the colonial settlers must be able to cover more ground by pushing further into the landscape. J. B. Jackson theorizes that the white settlers in the US solved the issue of how to make enforceable boundaries for their spaces with the invention of barbed wire in 1874. Now, instead of labor-intensive and difficult-to-move boundaries such as hedges, fences, trenches, and sod walls, barbed wire allows for an effective and easy-to-assemble and reassemble boundary—which comes with the bonus of being hard to see and injurious to those attempted to cross it. The implementation of barbed wire makes it possible for settler farms to grow. Barns also change in the Midwest around the same time. The balloon-frame barn is easy to construct, disassemble, and reassemble quickly with minimal skill, leading to the ability to disregard natural boundaries and push further into the landscape.

Barns become easier to construct, requiring fewer people, and cheaper to manufacture, so more people build them. As more barns pop up on the land, they become common in the landscape. Because they are everyday structures, the people around them quickly have experiences in them, emotional moments that form memories and attachments to the barns. And thus a mindset forms that justifies and sustains the material act of settling the land. This way of thinking arises from the foundational view of land as ownable and performs a vanishing act—veiling any thought that an original violence has ever been enacted. Colonial settlers build barns to house animals and equipment to farm to survive, not to push Native peoples off the lands, not to occupy the land. Boundaries must be protected for survival, not to keep those who don't own the land from the resources on it. Everything becomes about pushing forward.

This logic carries through to more mundane and even seemingly positive ways of viewing rural life. If only people cared about heritage and architecture and agriculture and folklore, they would save barns and farms. Farms are central to Americana, and as suburbs push further into rural land, we lose all that we were. The land can be held until the forests can be restored and the animals return, or at the very least, local farming can be implemented to feed rural residents. The land shouldn't be used for housing developments.

So we fight to keep barns as a way to preserve the landscape, the folkways, and the culture that came before, because the lived knowledges of that time feel ever more necessary in an increasingly technological, metropolitan world. Barns become symbols and metaphors inserted into discourses removed from their history, their context, the violence they were built for.

Nostalgia becomes a powerful fuel for this logic. I can go without seeing barns for months. I've gone my whole life without really tending to animals in them or using them for anything other than storage. I've never really farmed. And yet, when I see the barn behind my house that once protected animals inside fences framed by lilac bushes, I don't see it as a simple structure past its utility, decaying as all things decay. Instead, it becomes a container for my memories, a metaphor for my longing. This longing keeps me fighting to save some way of living I never really participated in, a way of living that has no influence on my life. The barn as symbol obscures what came before, justifies my feelings, keeps me in that time and place, perpetuating the logic. I become part of the machine that moves over the land, always forcefully shaping it.

My love for and wish to preserve the barns back home stems from a logic that sees the land as a site of abstraction. Onto the land I project a pristine vision of rurality. I can place my nostalgia, my fear of change, and the guilt I feel for leaving there. I can build a simple structure over them, fence it in, and keep close watch. From the land I can then extract comfort and safety, knowing that if the barns just stay standing, the old way of life I've spent all this time trying to write my way back to will be preserved. So long as they stay standing, I can learn everything I didn't in my youth and wait for the culture to change, so that when I slide open the doors there will be an Appalachia that's ready for me, that I'm ready for. But I know there's nothing left in those barns. And I know I need to give up the things that no longer serve me. I can allow symbols to lose their meaning. I must let structures crumble.

THE LINE SPINS THROUGH TIME

A series of round painted plaques hangs beside my front door. One depicts two red, yellow, green, and black distelfink, or thistle finches, facing each other above *Wilkum* written in Fraktur. Another shows a single blue thistle finch surrounded by hearts and flowers in bright blue, yellow, red, and green, above a heart with the inscription "Bless this House" written inside. Another has hand-painted red, white, green, and blue flowers with the inscription *Ein froher Gast ist niemals Last* (A happy guest is no one's trouble) written in Fraktur around the trim. The next is a carving of a tree and a pentagram, and the final one has a floral trim with "Home Sweet Appalachian Home" painted in blue and black inside the flower circle.

These plaques go by many names: hex signs, *hexafoos*, sechs signs, six signs, witch signs, barn stars, and *schtanne.* Along with barn quilts and Mail Pouch tobacco advertisements, barn stars decorate the large bank barns that fill the landscape of my home area in Ohio, which was settled by the Pennsylvania Dutch as they came west. German-language newspapers, and Lutheran, Methodist, and Pentecostal churches appeared in the region's towns with German names. Large Mennonite and Amish populations followed.

Hex signs are common enough that most people know what they are, but like me may not recall their origin or purpose. I'd never thought much about them growing up. I viewed them just as part of the vibrant, mundane surroundings of Southeast Ohio, something from another time that has stuck around, unexplained. I collect them because I appreciate their aesthetics and I know the symbols may be used for protection, as a prayer placed in the entryway of the home. But I don't know anything about their history or origin, and so maybe I'm missing something about my heritage and culture. I feel guilty sometimes when I find a new one and add it to my wall.

I have researched their symbolism. Most hex signs and barn stars are painted in red, yellow, and green, but blue is also prevalent. These colors are said to ward off sickness, spells, and witches. White symbolizes purity, strength, and everlasting life. Black symbolizes death while violet, which is rarely used, represents dignity, power, and humility. Yellow holds duality, meaning both degradation and jealousy and sacredness and divinity. Red symbolizes life, love, and hate, while green brings abundance and good fortune.

The colors of the signs complement the symbols painted on them. A shamrock brings good luck and an easy life. Oak leaves symbolize power as well as a strong body and mind. The distelfink, one of the most popular, is said to bring good luck or fortune. There are fertility hexes and sun, star, and rain hexes. There are rosette or love hexes and friendship hexes with tulips on them, which symbolize hope and charity. A sign with a large tulip and hearts stands for life and love. A double distelfink sign ensures love and marriage. There are also signs to bring plentiful harvests, peace and contentment, and power.

But I haven't carried out more than this superficial exploration. I realize there is an important distinction between appreciating barn signs for their decorative beauty and knowing their origin. As is true of many folkways and cultural artifacts, whether one knows the history seems to separate the old ways from the new, those who hold the tradition from those who don't. At the very least, knowing something's history means that you're "from somewhere," at least discursively. Functionally, for one who doesn't know the history and the context of the practices of one's area, the exercise of uncovering this information brings the living traditions of the past vibrantly into the present and connects one to one's area and heritage. So, to deepen my understanding, I delve into the history and cultural significance of hex signs. Hopefully they'll reflect something back to me about the culture I grew up in, something about me. At the very least, maybe I can reclaim something I missed growing up in the region.

Even a cursory investigation into the history and significance of hex signs uncovers a series of questions and competing discourses regarding their origin and importance. I encounter two main camps of thought regarding hexafoos. The first suggests that the signs are symbolic representations of folk religious culture and celestial symbols. Within this group, some believe the symbols are used mostly for protection and blessing, like talismans or amulets.

Plenty of testimonials from the mid-twentieth century apparently recorded this belief. In a special issue of *Pennsylvania Folklife* in 1960, Don Yoder cites a quote, supposedly from the *New York Times,* of a Pennsylvanian recounting the purpose of hex signs: "They're supposed to prevent the devil from entering the barn to give the cow milk fever." Another person confirms that the "arches painted on the front of Dutch barns are put there to make witches bump their heads when they attempt to fly into a barn!"

More testimonials collected from the time attest to the efficacy of the hex signs. Babies were born healthy, cows were healed, crops grew bountifully, and droughts were ended by abundant rain after people hung hexes. One testimonial was from a woman who, after years of struggling to conceive, was blessed with twins after hanging up a fertility hex. Asked if she thought her luck derived from the hex sign, she responded, "Yes it was . . . it gif me wonderful good results." Similarly, a man with rheumatism was cured of his knee pain by a healing hex.

Writers of the mid-twentieth century would have us believe that hex signs were endemic in the culture of the supposedly highly superstitious Pennsylvania Dutch. The Dutch would not have a barn without a hex sign present, just as they wouldn't walk under ladders, walk through graveyards on moonlit nights, or brag about being healthy without knocking on wood. They wouldn't let black cats cross their path, use the number 13, pass anyone on a street with a tree or bench in between them without saying "bread and butter," or break mirrors. Mid-twentieth century observers believed the hex sign motifs and designs dated back to cave paintings in Europe and had carried their meaning of warding off evil and bringing good luck unchanged through the centuries.

That belief, however, isn't shared by all. Some think that the real origin of barn stars traces back to celestial liturgical symbols, sacred geometry that has nothing to do with protecting the person who owns them. They're simply celebrations of heaven such as were found in Protestant Reformation churches that sought to separate themselves from the symbology of the Catholic Church. Thus, Protestants chose rosette stars over crucifixes and other symbols. The folk motifs and the belief in the power they hold are modern inventions.

The designs of schtanne still hold meaning, if not. A four-pointed star symbolizes the cross. The five-pointed star corresponds to the five wounds of Christ. The six-pointed star represents the six biblical days of creation; the seven-pointed star includes the Sabbath. The eight-pointed star symbolizes resurrection, and the nine-pointed star references the nine fruits of the spirit as told in Galatians. The twelve-pointed star relates to the twelve apostles, but also the twelve zodiac signs and the twelve months of the year.

The celestial symbols found in churches were also carved into the stone gables of barns, the stones and archways of houses, the arches of city gates, and were woven into the designs of house blessings. Traces of these designs—most notably the designs and motifs found on Swiss folk houses that combine inscriptions with family crests, celestial symbols, and geometric and liturgical designs—can be found on Pennsylvania barns. But the symbols on barns in Pennsylvania as well as the bank barn architecture itself were creations formed in the US in the nineteenth and twentieth centuries.

Some believe that since the bank barn design and the painting of stars on the broad side of barns are both relatively recent inventions, the argument that hex signs are some ancient traditions that are distinctly religious or magical in nature doesn't hold up. Moreover, barn stars, and to a lesser extent other motifs, have been found only on a small portion of barns in the Pennsylvania Dutch region, most of them within a thirty-mile radius of one town in one single county. The questions then arise as to why so few of the supposedly very superstitious Pennsylvania Dutch wanted to protect themselves from evil forces or bring blessings to their communities, and why only a handful of the religious majority wanted liturgical representations on their barns to celebrate God and heaven.

These questions lead to the second theory as to barn stars origin and purpose, which claims that the symbols are purely aesthetic, artistic creations that came about in a time and place wanting to celebrate and preserve rural life in a quickly industrializing world. There were known painters in the late nineteenth and mid-twentieth centuries who painted many barns in the Berks County region of Pennsylvania and left detailed records not only of the barns they painted but the number of hours spent painting and the recipes for the hand-made paints used in the process. A master craftsman would generally direct a crew of painters or apprentices to paint large stars on barns.

One such artist was Milton Hill, a prominent barn star craftsman in the twentieth century who painted barns throughout the Pennsylvania countryside. In the 1950s and '60s, the Kutztown Folk Festival offered tours of Dutch country so tourists could admire barn star artwork. Soon after, the director of the festival asked Milton Hill to paint barn stars on commercial sign boards so that the festival could display them without offering tours.

Eventually the popularity of barn stars led to their commercialization. Smaller hand-painted signs began to be sold at festivals and stores for people to hang on their barns or in their houses. The hex sign caught on most prominently when Johnny Ott, a craftsman who dubbed himself the "Professor of Hexology," began selling his ornate signs, featuring decorative folk imagery and celestial signs, as magical talismans. He spun tales of the magic and the power imbued in them, citing testimonials of those who had previously bought his signs. Ott had never painted signs on barns; he simply cashed in on their growing popularity.

Ott's tales followed the trend of broader tourist writing, or slumming literature, that was popular at the time. This type of writing set out to introduce "the other half," poor hardworking people, to the broader American public. It was hard to make such closed-off, industrious, plain people salacious, so writers transformed the Pennsylvania Dutch into a mysterious, otherworldly, extraordinary group of people. Thus, a simple decoration on a barn became magic. Many scholars now believe that many of the testimonials collected in the 1960s originated in Ott's stories.

The idea that the Pennsylvania Dutch culture was mysterious and superstitious arose even earlier, from the popular tourist literature of the 1920s and '30s. The name of the signs even came from travel writing of the time. The term hex sign came from the Pennsylvania Dutch word *hexafoos*, which was mistranslated as "witch's foot" by the Reverend Wallace Nutting. About the signs, he wrote:

> They are decoration sometimes applied on the door heads or on or about the door. They are supposed to be a continuance of a very ancient tradition, according to which these decorative marks were potent to protect the barn, or more particularly the cattle from the influence of witches. It is understood by those who are acquainted with witches that those ladies are particularly likely to harm cattle. As the wealth of the farmer was in his stock, contained in his remarkably substantial barn, the hexafoos was added to its decoration as a kind of spiritual or demoniac lightning rod!

The symbols the Reverend Nutting wrote about were likely not even the celestial symbols painted on the broad sides of barns but chalk symbols made ritually on the inside of barns. The makers of these chalk symbols didn't want to let outsiders document them. This refusal, combined with the reluctance of barn owners to explain the presumed functionality of the barn stars, might have led travel writers like Nutting to fill in the missing information with their own fantasies. He likely conflated the outward-facing brightly painted symbols on the barn with the ritual chalk symbols he saw painted inside, which are now believed to hold the function and meaning assigned to the painted plaques.

Not all travel writers of the time followed the line that the practices were superstitious, although their narratives were still stereotypical, describing the Pennsylvania Dutch as stubborn, hardworking, insular, defiantly stuck in the past, sternly religious, paradoxical, and enigmatic, unlike any other people in the country. Folklorists studying cultural practices during a time of deep change in the country portrayed the Pennsylvania Dutch similarly. In their ethnographies they transformed the practice of painting stars on barns into a piece of pure Americana, discrediting the belief there was any spiritual meaning behind the symbols. Scholars wrote that the signs were "just art"—or, as they claimed the Dutch said, "chust fer nice." To various writers at the time, therefore, the Pennsylvania Dutch were extraordinary either in their backward beliefs, or in their righteous plainness—but they were always extraordinary.

After researching the meaning and function of hex signs, I think they are some combination of decorative, symbolic, and functional. One would not build a house without doors, windows, walls and, in the case of the traditions passed down to the Dutch, a house blessing and possibly a symbolic inscription like a celestial symbol or folk motif. These symbols and inscriptions were an important part of the overall architectural plan that visually connected and completed the appearance and function of the structure. When the tradition came to Pennsylvania, it morphed and changed into a hybrid, like the barns the Dutch constructed in the new landscape. Hex signs, barn stars—whatever name they went by—were part of an everyday life in which the mundane and the sacred were woven together. The symbols aren't just part of some pure and unchanging cultural heritage, something ancient and mysterious, but something alive, ever changing as the world itself changes.

I planned to complete this essay with an explanation of the ways I deepened my connection to my home region, its spiritual and cultural identity, and the rural landscape and its artistic expressions, but I've cut the work short. The process of writing this has left me unfulfilled. I've lost some of the pleasure and wonder of admiring the hex signs in my house, and the excitement that once arose when I discovered a new design has faded. The magic is gone. On a deeper level, this research exhausted me because the questions and discourses I encountered in the process revealed an obvious parallel with the ones surrounding transgender existence, ones I've lost all patience for. Instead, I'll finish the essay by tracing this parallel through to show why I gave up on my mission midstream, why it was doomed from the beginning.

The questions and discourses I encounter about transgender existence most often center on origins. When did you first know? How long have you known? Did you always know? When did you come out? The questions aren't about me or my past; they seek to confirm and affirm the beliefs and assumptions the person asking them has about themselves and society—namely, that gender is something innate, relatively stable, and has a biological or even metaphysical basis. This false understanding originates from the belief that the earlier a person displays a trait, the more natural that trait must be. Our gender and sexuality must be innate from birth, or at the very least they manifest at the earliest possible moment, when as children we develop the language and understanding to be able to express them. These understandings supposedly comprise the core of who we are. We are born this way.

The born-this-way narrative, at its worst, can be used to invalidate transgender existence by claiming that the way we are at birth constitutes the way we will always be. At its best, the assumption that children come to know their gender at an early age—and may only be able to articulate it later— allows for but limits transgender identity to a narrow acceptable framework. Those of us who did not identify as transgender from a young age are seen as suspect and questioned or even outright invalidated. Some will say we haven't done the work to connect our identity to our backgrounds, that we must have missed the signs of our "true " identity. We were actually transgender all along.

The quest to write one's transgender story thus begins with rewriting one's past. We must transform our histories to fit a rigid narrative assigned to us, much the way our gender/sex assignment at birth shapes and limits the possible narratives of our entire future. Tracing gender or sexuality back to an origin doesn't consider how a person changes through time. Other facets of our identity change throughout time—our interests, our food preferences, our activity levels, our relationships, our friends, even our emotions and beliefs. The entire trajectory that leads to where we end up in life shifts as we grow older. But when it comes to gender or sexual identity, there's little room for a person to simply just change at some point in their life. This is part of the reason why people invest so heavily in questions about origins, because if there were other narratives, other possibilities, the asker of such questions could come to understand that their identities could have been and could still be otherwise. Encountering a transgender person whose narrative does not fit this acceptable mold destabilizes the fixedness of some people's understandings of gender, binary or not. The world as they believe it to be could collapse, so sticking to their beliefs, rooting into them, becomes easier.

The same quest to validate one's identity through tracing it back to an origin carries through to transgender as a phenomenon, as a way of living in the world. A transgender person must search for their origins in the past and discover the meaning and function of transness historically, and then in some way align their identity with this precedent. Transgender people were healers, rebels, peacemakers, divine beings, outlaws, wisdom keepers, warriors, and brave souls who moved between genders to accomplish a goal. They transformed, reinvented, disrupted the norm, or they navigated the system to live their truths. But they never just existed without serving some greater narrative function or purpose.

Transgender thus becomes a symbol that gets stuck in a double bind of representation. Trans disrupts the status quo, representing gender resistance and destabilization, while it also affirms the status quo, because people seem to go through physical and social transformation just to fit into the gender binary. There's no complexity, no depth, no ordinariness in such symbolism.

And no matter what a transgender person uncovers in their past, the information will likely fall short of fitting into a recognizable group identity because the experiences that shape us sometimes have nothing to do with that identity. And when this happens, we are required to look for a deeper meaning, as if we've missed the signs, misinterpreted them, or didn't go through the common experiences that should unite us. To align ourselves to the group identity, we must write and rewrite our stories into a unified ideal, whether or not that story is true to who we are.

In rewriting ourselves for a purpose, we conform to the structures of slumming literature. Just as rural slumming literature sought to reveal the secret mystical life of people like the Pennsylvania Dutch to confirm the stereotypes that the Dutch were stern, rigid, superstitious, and isolated from modernity, transgender and queer studies and literature have replicated this type of work through sexological studies, transgender memoirs, interviews, oral histories, and documentaries. A whole slew of media has been produced to make different transgender lives legible for a wide audience and to confirm or set straight the suspicions and beliefs of how the general public believes transgender people do or should live.

Rendering various forms of living legible for the mainstream offers no protection, no privacy, no right to interiority, no ability to be otherwise. We attempt to acknowledge, reclaim, and validate identities with the same logic, in the same categories, and with the same vocabulary by which we have been invalidated in the hope of some redemptive visibility. And we'll always fail at being understood and valued on our terms.

The origins of identity in terms of when it manifested in a person's life, or what place that identity, or experiences, traditions, and practices, holds in a person's life is not relevant to any sense of authenticity. What matters is that a behavior or practice or trait represents the vision a person has for themself and their future. And this backstory, the inner workings of how one comes to know oneself, does not need to be revealed for the sake of legibility. We don't need to know what's behind the closet or the barn door.

More than that, we can accept outright refusals to grant visibility for the sake of knowledge, no matter how curious we are, no matter the good we think such visibility might generate. We can acknowledge what we can discern, all that others willingly share with us, and honor a person's decision to let the rest of their life stay submerged or opaque without searching for some meaning to explicate for the sake of our own comfort.

The poet Fanny Howe writes that wanting to be noticed is not wanting to be found. "A signal does not necessarily mean that you want to be located or described. It can mean that you want to be known as Unlocatable and Hidden." She calls this experience of the personal that is unlocatable and hidden "bewilderment." "Bewilderment is an enchantment that follows a complete collapse of reference and reconcilability. It cracks open the dialectic and sees myriads all at once." When we are lost, unstable, unsure, everything in life opens and expands and we become able to wonder, able to think from within and beyond what can be readily understood. And if there's any hope in identity as a project, in all that we hold and practice to make sense of ourselves, whether we call it queer or transgender or Appalachian, it might be found in being bewildered, in forgoing knowability to bestow upon ourselves a complex interiority and wonderous possibility.

I don't care what transgender or Appalachian means or what they can do. I experience myself and my surroundings and all that's been passed down to me without needing to fit a mold, to fill a role, to be part of some compulsory group for the sake of a visibility that will never save me. I can be lost in myself, unsteady and uneasy, and remain vulnerable to the unknowing. In that place I still find connection.

So maybe I can finish this essay with deeper insight into myself after the exploration of hex signs. I don't care what their meaning or function is. I don't care what they represent. I want to appreciate them when I see them on the entry stones of doors, on gates and archways, on the broad sides of barns, in the doorway of my home. I want to appreciate their celestial and pastoral designs and imagine that, like them, I and my gender and my identity, all the vastness and mundanity that has brought me into being, can one day just become part of the everyday architecture.

Homeplace

Fettered steps. Whirl of dust around dangling front legs embedded in dirt pushed by tiny trembling back ones. Flat trails leading back to themselves like a thought cut short, never reaching a destination, never having a destination at all. The partially paralyzed calf was repulsive, Donnie thought. Not repulsive—he was struck with guilt and sadness—the contempt was merely a deflection. Pathetic, the calf was pathetic. Donnie rose every morning before dawn and fed the animals, collected the eggs, milked the cows, and cleaned the stalls. Finally, as the cinnabar sky dripped black, he tossed hay into the calf's pen before quickly returning to the house.

Donnie's mother was an efficient butcher and a fine cook. On Sundays she always cooked a special meal. *Momma's favorite was veal, and she loved brains the most.* Donnie shut his eyes tight on the word *loved* as his voice shot up high. The wrinkles on his forehead testified to the depth of his memory. *We all liked tripe and offal, you see, but no one else, no one else would touch the brains. She said it felt like butter and tasted like roast chestnuts.* Donnie's hoarse laugh accented his words with a deep staccato.

One Sunday after church, Donnie swallowed hard as he passed his mother in the kitchen prepping Sunday dinner. He wrestled with the truth in his stomach as he approached the table to find what he knew was there: veal, Mother's favorite meal. He had not seen the calf in the pen that morning. He stared at the plate of meat covered in viscous brown gravy. All he could see were shaking limbs pushed in dirt, creating circles in the ground like the peppered gravy on the platter. He couldn't eat it, but he knew he had to. Donnie stared down at his feet, desperately wrestling with possible ways he could leave the table without offending his mother. Pulling hard at the pins transfixing his gaze to his shoes, he saw that his mother's plate was stacked with potatoes but not the veal.

Donnie had never once seen his mother not eat meat, not with the Depression a mere decade behind them. She was resolute, the foundation upon which the thirteen-person family rested. He never knew her as a woman who would shy away from a hard decision or feel deeply toward an animal whose sole purpose was to provide food. But he knew she too saw the shaking calf as she looked at the plate of veal. Touched by her tenderness but not wanting to draw attention to it, he passed her the green beans in silence and started in on his potatoes, careful to avoid the gravy.

Brown cotton twine scratching butcher paper. Efficient hands moving with speed tying bows around slabs of carefully wrapped pork. Slabs stacked neatly into rows in the cooler.

If you take the time to make bows you don't have to cut the twine and you can reuse it. No sense in buying more, Elaine informed me.

She just brought two of her pigs in for slaughter, the meat from which would provide her four-person family with enough food for winter. Elaine had raised animals for food since she was a girl. There was no hesitation in her thoughts, no trepidation as she tended to them, even thought she knew their death was imminent.

When her son was young, she bought him a small black pig. He'd raise the pig for show, and when the time came take her for slaughter. This was a life lesson: the food chain, the Circle of Life, living with and from the flesh of animals. Folk knowledge instilled; livelihood passed on. He took his pig to 4-H competitions and to county fairs and she won many blue ribbons, as expected. But he named her and grew close to her. Elaine did too. When the time came to take the pig to slaughter, she couldn't do it. And so Miss Piggy became the center of stories told at holiday gatherings for another decade.

There exists a deeply rooted and rarely questioned folk wisdom in the country regarding animals. This knowledge contains a hierarchy of creatures that extends from pets at the pinnacle to animals that exist for food somewhere in the center to rodents and insects at the base. No matter where the animals fall on the hierarchy, if they are injured or beyond their economic usefulness they are mercy-killed. Plenty of colloquialisms attest to this worldview, some used literally, others as metaphors: *Take the dog out back. Sometimes you gotta shoot a horse in the head. Take 'em out behind the barn.*

As I grew up, this worldview informed my thinking; when confronted with my own suffering, my attention quickly turned to how I could place each element in a hierarchy of importance. Things at the bottom of the ladder were easiest to ignore—experiencing discomfort in social situations, my dissatisfaction with how I looked, having to conceal myself. In the middle I placed family and friends I hadn't come out to who I could cut out of my life to avoid dealing with the dissonance. At the top of the hierarchy, gender dysphoria hovered thick, clinging to me no matter how far down I tried to force it. Killing my suffering became a mission that I soon conflated with comfort, because it was easier than affirming or dealing with my issues.

The American Veterinary Medical Association provides guidelines for mercy killings. I turned to the guiding questions instinctively. To determine whether a mercy killing will ease suffering, one must ask a series of questions. Will the medical condition result in a lifetime of confinement? Does the immediate medical condition contain a hopeless prognosis? Is the animal a hazard to itself or to humans? Will the animal require medication for the remainder of its life?

I saw these conditions laid out before me. I thought I wouldn't survive staying at home socially, and I was an enemy to my body. I figured at best I'd become a medicated specter. Escape might ease my pain. I hoped to rid myself of all that was stifling me. I could drive away and let it all dissolve in the phantom fields that led to the big city, in the red of brake lights on the dark-rain pavement, in the black diesel plumes waiting for someone to become entrapped in their suffocating embrace.

I sought refuge in the metropolis, in the many anonymous houses and buildings laid out in grids like poorly planned fields. I changed the way I lived. I changed the way I dressed, I found new interests and ways to carry myself. I was looking for anonymity, to finally not be different in a place with so many other transgender people. I found not anonymity but erasure. The infinite walls of the cityscape closed off all possibility the body inside their confines longed for.

I learned of another list while living in the city that might relieve the pain I held. The World Professional Association for Transgender Health provides guidelines for transgender individuals to ease their suffering. They suggest making changes to our gender expression and role to alleviate social discomfort, seeking medication in the form of hormone therapy, seeking surgery to alter our bodies to ease dysphoria, and undergoing psychotherapy to improve our body image and our social support networks.

I followed the list too, hoping that after changing everything about myself, I would be rid of my discomfort. I used medication to reshape my biology. I went to therapy and I met others with whom I could share these formerly closed-off parts of myself. And some parts of my life did improve, but I was still fractured. I was lost and I could find no home, no feeling of belonging that I could cling to, no foundation that could support the tenderness I craved.

I longed to patch the seams of my split worlds into a quilt of my own design. What seemed the inevitable starting point of my search was genealogy, a way to trace back the lines to construct a haunted continuity. I collected stories from relatives I admired hoping to find the tenderness I sought, but I found only brief tender moments in the memories, fleeting fragments. I could inhabit neither the world of these memories nor the confines of the metropolis. I needed space in which I could live as unencumbered as I could in any field, protected by trees, away from prying eyes. I wanted a space for resistance, for healing, for renewal, a place in which I could be whole.

The volunteer at the sanctuary gate greets me with a wave. He tries to wipe some of the mud and grass from his hand before shaking mine, but it's not necessary. Something in the transfer of soil, of sweat, of work, is powerful and comforting. The gate creaks as it opens, and the chain that holds it shut breaks away and bounces, muffled, on its weathered post. Smooth aster and purple coneflower have overtaken the space around the signpost, obscuring the name of the sanctuary: Sunrise. It is almost noon and already stiflingly hot. The humid air sticks to every surface and carries with it the smell of dirt and hay, wildflower and field. I approach the first row of weathered bank barns to see some of the animals living here.

Fettered steps. Whirl of dust around dangling back legs embedded in dirt pulled by tiny trembling front ones. The goat kid, its hind legs paralyzed, pulls itself through the dirt to the fence to greet me. The rough hairs around his eyes feel like boot brushes and his tiny curlicue horns are as smooth as a polished railing. From behind, a potbellied pig brushes against my knees, making them buckle. I turn and stand to survey the property. This place defies conventional wisdom. The animals have names; they are free from hierarchies of worth and consumption. Most have outlived their economic usefulness, and many have sustained injuries that most would find worthy of mercy killings. Yet the mercy here derives not from pity but from dignity, a tender acknowledgment. There are no walls to close off possibility, no inherited knowledge or lists to outline paths for behavior. The shelter allows for space to resist, to heal, to renew, to be whole.

The day passes on, but the heat is sustained. Most of the animals have crowded into the barns to rest in the shade under the fans. I'm in the largest barn, wetting towels to put on the backs of the steer to keep them cool under the fans. The biggest is seven feet at his rear haunches. Trying to get the towel spread out without it falling off feels like a challenging game of tag, one I repeatedly lose. I take a break to get water and rest my shoulders. In the grass-specked water of the cattle tub I see my reflection. I have changed. The way I dress, the way I carry myself, the way I speak are different from when I fled a place like this. But I don't look out of place. My body fills the empty space left by killing and rupturing.

The steer licks my face, shaking me from my contemplation. I lean in, place a freshly wet towel on his tall shoulders, and rub his neck under his chin, making him shake his head and snort. I step away and wipe the saliva away with my forearm, creating a swirl of dirt on my face. I see my reflection again. The dirt accentuates the unique contours of my face, tracing the edges of my lips, up through the bridge of my nose, and past my forehead to my hairline before stopping like a thought cut short, never reaching its destination, never having a destination at all.

ACKNOWLEDGMENTS

My deepest thanks to my editor Abby Freeland for championing the book when it was an idea in a tweet, and for guiding it to completion, even through my constant doubt. I'm grateful to Ashley Runyon, the team at UPK, and the Appalachian Futures series editors Annette Saunooke Clapsaddle, Davis Shoulders, and Crystal Wilkinson. Thank you for choosing my book and for your hard work in turning my raw materials into a tangible product. Thank you to the two gracious peer reviewers whose feedback shaped the book.

The Taft Research Center and the Department of Women's, Gender, and Sexuality Studies at the University of Cincinnati provided grants and fellowships that allowed me the time, money, and space to write my MA thesis, which became the foundation of this book. Thank you for championing interdisciplinary and creative work and for your encouragement. A special shoutout to all ten members of my Ride or Die MA cohort.

I'm so grateful that my time in Cincinnati overlapped with that of my mentor, co-conspirator, and dear friend J. T. Roane. I'm not sure what I'd be thinking or writing without your challenging and productive conversations, feedback, and edits, but it couldn't have resulted in this book.

Two essays in this book were previously published, and I'm so happy to have worked with the strong editors who gave them a home: Ryan Schuessler and Kevin Whiteneir Jr. included "Lancaster Is Burning" in their *Sweeter Voices Still* anthology, and Ryan Schnurr featured the essay in *Belt Magazine*; Cameron Awkward Rich chose

"Homeplace: Sunrise" (titled "Homeplace" here) for *Heart Online Journal* (RIP).

I have very many fellow writers to thank, and I hope I name you all here. Jodi Rath was my first true champion. Thanks for your wisdom, for writing by example, for bringing kindness and literature to our horribly underfunded and drab school, and for your unyielding support. My group chat gals, Emily Brier, Eileen Elizabeth Espinoza, and Amanda Page, have given me daily sanity through many conversations on writing as well as feedback on this book. For commentary on early drafts of some of these essays, thank you to Emma Hudelson, Raechel Anne Jolie, Zefyr Lisowski, and to Kirsten Iversen and my pals from her 2018 literary nonfiction workshop Kathleen, Emily, Claire, and Mike. Thank you to Carter Sickels for offering constant support and for paving the trans Appalachian writer path in front of me. Alison Stine—I am still trying to become you when I grow up.

The *Lancaster Eagle Gazette* has for some reason very closely documented my family over the last century, and I'm grateful for being able to access such a rich archival history.

If we have been friends anytime during my life, you might have ended up in this book. I'm particularly glad to still be friends with the characters I have called Lux and Levi, even if we're all far away from the hills. This book couldn't have happened without the family members who raised me and whose stories I have shared in this book. Bessie, Beatrice, William, Donnie, LaDonna, Dolores, Sharon, and Jeanine—you are gone but I hope I've honored your legacy. An eternal thanks to my aunt Elaine for inspiring my love of archival research and family history, and to my cousin Shelley for her support. To all my Grover family: you are in this book in spirit even if you're not named, and naming all of you would eat up my word count. Thank you for the life you've given me, for your love and for your stories. I still cherish you all.

I signed my contract and wrote much of this book during the many weekly dinners hosted by my reality television dinner and video game/board game pals Matt and Bill. Thank you for putting up with me.

Sonny—I'm not sure if home would have ever been home without you. You've been gone almost ten years, but I hope to keep you alive for as long as I can in writing. Your family will always be my family.

Finally, and most importantly, I am grateful to my partner, constant companion, cat mom, best friend, intellectual sparring partner, personal photographer, German translator, and artist extraordinaire Elizabeth. Thank you for buying me that Moleskine ten years ago when I said I wanted to write again.

BIBLIOGRAPHY

Alexander, Brian. *Glass House: The 1% Economy and the Shattering of the All-American Town.* New York: St. Martin's, 2017.

American Veterinary Association. *AMVA Guidelines for the Euthanasia of Animals.* 2020. https://www.avma.org/sites/default/files/2020-02/Guidelines-on-Euthanasia-2020.pdf.

Anglin, Mary. "Erasures of the Past: Culture, Power, and Heterogeneity in Appalachia." *Journal of Appalachian Studies* 10, nos. 1–2 (2004): 73–84.

Appalachian Regional Commission. https://www.arc.gov/.

Behar, Ruth. *The Vulnerable Observer: Anthropology That Breaks Your Heart.* Boston: Beacon, 1997.

Berlant, Lauren. *Cruel Optimism.* Durham, NC: Duke University Press, 2011.

Bowman, Samuel M., and Richard B. Irwin. *Sherman and His Campaigns.* New York: Charles Richardson, 1865.

Brody, Jane. "Benefits of Transsexual Surgery Disputed as Leading Hospital Halts the Procedure." *New York Times,* October 2, 1979. https://www.nytimes.com/1979/10/02/archives/benefits-of-transsexual-surgery-disputed-as-leading-hospital-halts.html.

Campbell, Will D. *Brother to a Dragonfly.* New York: Seabury, 1977.

Carrie Buck v. John Hendren Bell, Superintendent of State Colony for Epileptics and Feeble Minded. 274 U.S. 200 (1927).

Chrissman, James. *Death and Dying in Central Appalachia: Changing Attitudes and Practices.* Champaign: University of Illinois Press, 1994.

Diagnostic and Statistical Manual of Mental Disorders. 4th and 5th eds. Washington, DC: American Psychiatric Association, 1994, 2013.

Dickens, Charles. *Hard Times.* New York: T. L. McElrath, 1854.

"Dolores Pitches in at Fair." *Lancaster Eagle Gazette,* October 14, 1954.

Donmoyer, Patrick. *Hex Signs: Myth and Meaning in Pennsylvania Dutch Barn Stars.* Kutztown: Pennsylvania German Cultural Heritage Center, Kutztown University, 2013.

Dunaway, Wilma. *The First American Frontier: Transition to Capitalism in Southern Appalachia, 1700–1860.* Chapel Hill: University of North Carolina Press, 2000.

Eugenics Records Office. https://www.cshl.edu/archives/institutional-collections /eugenics-record-office/.

Fawcett, John. dir. *Ginger Snaps*. Toronto: 20th Century Fox, 2000.

"Garden Club at Carroll Hostess for Flower Show." *Lancaster Eagle Gazette*, October 27, 1951.

"Golden Wedding Anniversary Set." *Lancaster Eagle Gazette*, July 20, 1984.

Gómez-Barris, Macarena. *The Extractive Zone: Social Ecologies and Decolonial Perspectives*. Durham, NC: Duke University Press, 2017.

Gumbs, Alexis Pauline. *Spill: Scenes of Black Feminist Fugitivity*. Durham, NC: Duke University Press, 2016.

Halberstam, Jack. *The Queer Art of Failure*. Durham, NC: Duke University Press, 2011.

Hines, J. T. Herrera. *Hexology: The Art and Meaning of The Pennsylvania Dutch Hex Symbols*. York: York Pennsylvania Press, 1964.

Holmes, Roy Hinman. *The Farm in a Democracy*. Ann Arbor, MI: Edwards Bros., 1922.

Howe, Fanny. "Bewilderment." *How(2) Journal* 1, no. 1 (1999). https://www.asu .edu/pipercwcenter/how2journal/archive/online_archive/v1_1_1999/fhbewild .html.

Jackson, John Brinckerhoff. *Landscape in Sight: Looking at America*. Edited by Helen Lefkowitz Horowitz. New Haven, CT: Yale University Press, 1997.

Johnson, Jessica Marie. "'We Need Your Freedom': An Interview with Alexis Pauline Gumbs." *Black Perspectives*. AAIHS, December 13, 2016. https://www .aaihs.org/we-need-your-freedom-an-interview-with-alexis-pauline-gumbs/.

Kephart, Horace. *Our Southern Highlanders: A Narrative of Adventure in the Southern Appalachians and a Study of Life among the Mountaineers*. Rev. ed. New York:Macmillan, 1922.

Lewis, Oscar. *Five Families: Mexican Case Studies in the Culture of Poverty*. New York: Basic Books, 1959.

"A Little Cincinnati Boy." *Delaware County Daily Times*, June 10, 1881.

Love, Heather. *Feeling Backwards: Loss and the Politics of Queer History*. Cambridge, MA: Harvard University Press, 2009.

"Mainly about People." *Lancaster Eagle Gazette*, July 27, 1951.

"Members Replace 4-H Girl's Show Saddle Burned in Fire." *Lancaster Eagle Gazette*, September 22, 1961.

"The Middle West Farm Woman of Today Is the Man of the Family." *Washington Post*, n.d., 1923.

Nichols, George Ward. *The Story of the Great March: From the Diary of a Staff Officer.* New York: Harper and Brothers, 1865.

Nutting, Wallace. *Pennsylvania Beautiful.* Framingham, MA: Old America, 1924.

Peitzmeier, Sarah M. et al. "Intimate Partner Violence in Transgender Populations: Systematic Review and Meta-analysis of Prevalence and Correlates." *American Journal of Public Health* 110, no. 9 (2020): e1–e14.

Rich, Frank. "No More Sympathy for the Hillbilly." *New York Magazine,* March 2017. https://nymag.com/intelligencer/2017/03/frank-rich-no-sympathy-for-the-hillbilly.html.

Rosenberg, Gabriel. *4-H Harvest: Sexuality and the State in Rural America.* Philadelphia: University of Pennsylvania Press, 2015.

Sanderson, Esther Sharp. *County Scott and Its Mountain Folk.* Huntsville, TN: Esther Sharp Sanderson, 1958.

Sanderson, George. *A Brief History of the Early Settlement of Fairfield County: Being the Substance of a Lecture Delivered before the Lancaster Literary Institute: With Additional Facts.* Lancaster, OH: Lancaster Literary Institute, 1851.

Satterwhite, Emily. "Intro to Appalachian Studies: Navigating the Myths of Appalachian Exceptionalism." In *Appalachia in the Classroom: Teaching the Region,* edited by Theresa L. Burriss and Patricia M. Gantt. Athens Ohio University Press, 2013.

Scalf, Henry P. "The Death and Burial of 'Boney Bill' Scalf." *Appalachian Heritage* 2, no. 2 (1974): 57–60.

Sedgwick, Eve Kosofsky. *Touching Feeling: Affect, Pedagogy, Performativity.* Durham, NC: Duke University Press, 2003.

Skidmore, Emily. *True Sex: The Lives of Trans Men at the Turn of the Twentieth Century.* New York: NYU Press, 2017.

Sontag, Susan. *Against Interpretation.* 1966. Reprint, New York: Farrar, Straus, and Giroux, 2013.

Stone, Sandy. "The *Empire* Strikes Back: A Post-Transsexual Manifesto." In *Body Guards: The Cultural Politics of Gender Ambiguity,* edited by Kristina Straub and Julia Epstein. London: Routledge, 1991.

"Superstition." *Cincinnati Daily Gazette,* June 24, 1868.

Tolentino, Jia. "The Personal-Essay Boom Is Over." *New Yorker,* May 18, 2017. https://www.newyorker.com/culture/jia-tolentino/the-personal-essay-boom-is-over.

Walz, E. L. *The Complete Explanation of the Calendar, with a Comprehensive Instruction of the Heavenly Bodies.* Reading, PA: Johann Ritter, 1830.

Weston, Kath. "Get Thee to a Big City: Sexual Imaginary and the Great Gay Migration." *GLQ* 2, no. 3 (1995): 253–77.

"A Witch Wreath." *Cincinnati Enquirer,* March 12, 1898.

World Professional Association for Transgender Health. *Standards of Care for the Health of Transsexual, Transgender, and Gender Nonconforming People.* 7th ed. 2012. https://www.wpath.org/publications/soc.

Yoder, Don. "Plain Dutch and Gay Dutch: Two Worlds in the Dutch Country." *Pennsylvania Folklife* Special Festival Issue (Summer 1960). https://digitalcommons.ursinus.edu/pafolklifemag/9.

Yoder, Don, and Thomas E. Graves. *Hex Signs: Pennsylvania Dutch Barn Symbols & Their Meaning.* 2nd ed. Mechanicsburg, PA: Stackpole Books, 2000.

APPALACHIAN FUTURES
Black, Native, and Queer Voices

SERIES EDITORS
Annette Saunooke Clapsaddle, Davis Shoulders, and Crystal Wilkinson

A book series that gives voice to Black, Native, Latinx, Asian, Queer, and other nonwhite or ignored identities within the Appalachian region.